# Working With Schizophrenia

## A Needs Based Approach

of related interest

**Psychosis: Understanding and Treatment**
*Edited by Jane Ellwood*
ISBN 1 85302 265 9

**Mental Health at Work**
*Edited by Michael Floyd, Margery Povall and Graham Watson*
ISBN 1 85302 177 6
*Disability and Rehabilitation Series 5*

**Good Practice in Supervision**
**Statutory and Voluntary Organisations**
Edited by Jacki Pritchard
ISBN 1 85302 279 9

**Shakespeare as Prompter**
**The Amending Imagination and the Therapeutic Process**
*Edited by Murray Cox and Alice Theilgaard*
ISBN 1 85302 159 8

**Community Care Practice and the Law**
*Edited by Michael Mandelstam with Belinda Schwehr*
ISBN 1 85302 273 X

# Working With Schizophrenia
## A Needs Based Approach

*Gwen Howe*
*Foreword by Kathleen Jones*

Jessica Kingsley Publishers
London and Bristol, Pennsylvania

First published in the United Kingdom in 1995 by

Jessica Kingsley Publishers Ltd

116 Pentonville Road

London N1 9JB, England

and

1900 Frost Road, Suite 101

Bristol, PA 19007, U S A

**Library of Congress Cataloging in Publication Data**

A CIP catalogue record for this book is available from the Library of Congress

**British Library Cataloguing in Publication Data**

A CIP catalogue record for this book is available from the British Library

ISBN 1 85302 242 X

Printed and Bound in Great Britain by

Cromwell Press, Melksham, Wiltshire

# Contents

# III: A Needs Based Approach

# IV: A Way Forward

This book is dedicated to all those families who have to struggle for survival because of the ignorance surrounding the handling of this illness

# Acknowledgements

This book has come about because courageous and valued friends have been prepared to share their pains and triumphs in order to benefit others still struggling with schizophrenia. I am indebted to them for their honesty and generosity. Four decided to contribute under a name other than their own and the rest were happy 'to go public'. I have, nevertheless, decided after some deliberation to omit surnames of sufferers and most carers just in case some day any one of them might feel exploited by my enthusiasm to share their experiences with my colleagues working in the mental health field. If I prove to be wrong about this, then any future editions will rectify this! Meanwhile, an enormous thank you to:

Julie Barnett, Ena Coulter, Bella Faulkner, Graham, Jan, Jill, Mary and Bill, Betty McMeekin, Heather Murray, Pat, Ralph, Sally, Stephen and Tina.

A big thank you too to everyone who makes up the small community we call St Paul's and in particular to its superb team of voluntary workers, to the members of the local NSF group and to the other dedicated people who have supported this project and, indirectly, this book.

My thanks once again to my family for their patience and good humour while I seemingly take on an impossible number of projects at any one time.

Finally, my gratitude to Kathleen Jones for her support and for her invaluable criticism of three of the chapters in this book.

# Foreword

Many people shy away from the word 'schizophrenia': the fact remains that it is the only word we have to describe patterns of thought and behaviour disorder which affect about one person in a hundred in every society. Given appropriate medication and adequate social support, most people with schizophrenia can now live in the community; but in the present state of research, we know much more about medication than we do about the kinds of social support they need.

Patients, clients, users, sufferers – we do not even have an agreed term to describe them. Gwen Howe calls them sufferers: she makes it clear that what they want from life is what the rest of us want – a home, a family circle, enough money to get by, friends, occupation and a sense of belonging; but the condition can be isolating and disabling – and relatives, with the best will in the world, may be unable to cope. Often, they find themselves living under intense strain, their own lives disrupted by problems beyond their capacity to deal with alone.

Gwen Howe starts by describing what schizophrenia means to chronic sufferers and their families; how they often face lack of communication from professionals, lack of understanding from health and social services, and prejudice and denial from the general public – even from one leading voluntary mental health organisation, which should know better.

She goes on to provide a needs-based analysis: many of her case-studies have been provided by people with schizophrenia and their relatives. They illustrate the need for information and explanation, common problems and how they can be faced, strategies for avoiding crises or dealing with crises, and damage limitation. There is a model scheme for providing social support which could be followed by statutory and voluntary agencies in other areas.

This is a practical book, written without jargon, and without pretension, and based on the author's extensive working experience. It emphasises the importance of listening to sufferers and their relatives, respecting their emotional reactions and their formulations of their difficulties, and helping them to reach their own solutions. It is underscored by a passionate belief in human rights, and in the potential of people with schizophrenia to attain a better quality of life than many find possible.

The book will be valuable to many people for the detailed information it contains, the understanding of human dilemmas which it conveys, and the humanity with which it is written. It should be standard reading for professionals in the mental health services. Voluntary workers and families trying to help a person with schizophrenia will find in it much that they need to know; and many sufferers will find it a source of support and assistance, as they try to cope with their own problems, and the day-to-day stresses in their lives.

Kathleen Jones
*Emeritus Professor of Social Policy*
*University of York*

# Introduction

I hope *Working with Schizophrenia* will serve as a practical handbook for mental health professionals and others trying to help the victims of this illness to find a reasonable quality of life in the community.

Following the publication of my last book, *The Reality of Schizophrenia* (Faber & Faber 1991), the Policy Director of MIND wrote a condemning review for this, concluding with 'in this field lasting solutions can only be found by engaging with the middle ground of philosophical and ethical complexity'.[1]

I feel this comment highlights rather well the whole debate surrounding schizophrenia. For many decades, this has indulged itself in considering such matters at the expense of addressing itself to the harsh realities of a common illness. Moreover, the debate strays so far from such practical matters that it even engages periodically in considering whether schizophrenia actually exists or whether it is 'a myth'. For example, the ideas of the late R.D. Laing have had a profound influence on British social work training over several decades and he remains something of a 'guru' for many professionals. He pronounced schizophrenia to be an appropriate response to unacceptable pressures from society and from families in particular. Such ideas have never been substantiated and, more important, R.D. Laing seemed to have difficulty identifying them, let alone understanding them, himself. He commented in 1982:

> 'I don't think I could pass an exam question on what is R.D. Laing's theory. I was looked to as one who had the answers but I never had them'[2]

Not surprisingly, this sort of debate has done nothing to improve the quality of life for sufferers or for those who love them. If you or yours suffered from a potentially damaging illness, would you be looking for literature that concerned itself with 'the middle ground of philosophical and ethical complexity' in the debate surrounding that illness? Similarly, would you be hoping that those paid to work with schizophrenia were concerning themselves with such matters? Do you know any other illness in which this would be the case?

It has seemed to many of us who specialize in working with serious mental illness that it is high time that we started to redress the balance and *The Reality of Schizophrenia* was dedicated to doing just that. All but two of its reviewers recognized the reality I have described. *Working with Schizophrenia* is again concerned with reality; the harsh reality as those most affected by the illness experience it. It is also concerned with finding and sharing ways to cope with this reality.

Happily, sufferers and carers have made a large contribution to the book and I feel very privileged that they should want to do this and hope that others will be encouraged to do the same. It is they who have developed something of a monopoly of expertise on this subject while the ongoing academic debate has concerned itself with other things. We all have much to learn from the victims of this illness and it has now become a matter of urgency that we should start to do this. It is quite evident that community care has so far failed to protect the interests of those sufferers who are most at risk, as well as the interests of others involved in their personal tragedies. In these circumstances, the stigma, fear, and ignorance which surrounds serious mental illness can only escalate, together with the pain of all the brave individuals trying to get on with 'life after schizophrenia'.

As in my previous books, I have to say once again that I hope that the use of the word 'sufferer' will not upset some individuals who object to this word. As I have explained before, I find it every bit as inappropriate to call people 'schizophrenics' as to call others 'broken legs' or 'irritable bowel syndromes'. When I say 'user', a fashionable term which is very much part of the jargon surrounding community care issues, most of the sufferers I know object to this. Two of them, Sally and Tina, have contributed to this book. Sally feels that the word is inextricably associated with drug abuse and Tina tells me that the word 'user' has connotations for her of 'being used' rather than listened to; summing up her frustrating experience of 'user involvement' exercises. So, once again, I hope those who do not like the word 'sufferer' will bear with me and take note that we haven't yet found a word which will keep most of the people happy most of the time.

Gwen Howe, March 1994

# I
# About Schizophrenia

CHAPTER 1

# Reality, Not Myth!

'Mr Ash is worried about his wife – could you pop out and see her? She's schizophrenic and manages quite well although she hears voices all the time. Find out if the voices are being friendly. If they're bullying her or telling her to kill herself, try and persuade her to come into hospital'

This was the mid 1970s and I was a raw recruit to both social work and the concepts of psychiatry. Those few sentences from my teamleader were the only training offered me on this serious illness before I was let loose on some of the most traumatized individuals and families in our society. Fortunately for me – and for them – the sufferers I worked with turned out to be excellent teachers, as did some of those who love them.

As for Mrs Ash, she represented my first contact with schizophrenia; one I would not forget. This was a level of personal torment and pain that was new to me and my feelings of inadequacy became irrelevant in the face of this woman's quiet courage. I started down a road of discovery that morning that led to a growing determination to find ways to to combat the misery of this illness.

Two decades on, I frequently meet new mental health professionals whose lack of training on this subject seems very much to reflect my own experiences. The English and Welsh National Boards Training Syllabus of 1982 highlighted the need for a *change from a medical model to a social model*[1] and psychiatric nursing students can now successfully complete a three-year training course without learning about schizophrenia in any real depth. and without mention of the subject in their examination papers. Similarly, a survey[2] which assessed the value of the training for approved social workers (ASWs), who play a key role in mental health assessments, found that the social workers themselves did not feel that they knew enough about the mentally ill and matters concerning the mentally ill. Psychiatric nurses and ASWs play key roles in the lives of schizophrenia sufferers, but so do many untrained staff out in the community who are expected to work with this illness without any real knowledge of what it is all about or how it affects its victims. Yet we are talking about the most serious of the mental illnesses and one which took up two-thirds of long-term hospital beds before the run-down of the mental hospitals.

What other basic facts should we note about this illness or, perhaps more accurately, group of illnesses with a classic cluster of symptoms?

## About Schizophrenia

Schizophrenia is a psychotic condition in which sufferers can lose touch with reality to an extent where they believe they are neither ill nor in need of treatment. For this reason – and because of the sort of denial and ignorance seemingly reflected in professional training programmes – people with schizophrenia can be left untreated, and this can lead to wasted lives and to family breakdown.

The incidence of schizophrenia is so common and persistent that one in every one hundred of us worldwide can expect to have a schizophrenic illness during our lifetime. The chances, however, fade with age as it attacks eighty per cent of its victims for the first time when they are in the prime of life, between the ages of 16 and 25 years.

Schizophrenia is treatable and, as for all other illnesses, the earlier it is caught the better the outcome is likely to be. Richard Wyatt's comprehensive summary of relevant research on this subject sums this up:

> 'some patients are left with a damaging residual if a psychosis is allowed to proceed unmitigated. While psychosis is undoubtedly demoralizing and stigmatizing, it may also be biologically toxic'[3]

Most sufferers will need a mix of medical and social care. So far as we know, although treatable, the illness is not curable; everyone who has a schizophrenic breakdown remains vulnerable to further attacks, although around twenty-five per cent will not, in fact, relapse.

The illness accounts for the majority of 'revolving door' admissions to hospital in which patients recover and then relapse, and these take up nine beds for every one taken up by a new diagnosed sufferer.[4] Some individuals slip into the chronic form of the illness, perhaps after a second or later breakdown; this is a seriously debilitating condition.

## A Discrepancy

There would seem to be a real discrepancy between the potential burden this illness imposes on the health services and the importance given to it in the professional training of those providing these services. Not surprisingly, there is a similarly wide gap between service providers' understanding of schizophrenia and the reality experienced by sufferers and relatives. A framework of provision has developed which has been shaped by academic debate, civil liberties ideology and economic considerations rather than by any appreciation or consideration of the needs of those having to cope with schizophrenia in the community. In fact, service providers' energies and resources have increasingly been absorbed on matters that have very low priority for the majority of those affected by the potential ravages of this illness.

Sufferers and carers alike despair about the lack of practical, constructive, care available to them while many of those employed to work with this illness find themselves more and more discouraged by the absence of really effective measures with which to help their clients. Perhaps it is not surprising that many professionals and other service providers tend to find working with this type of illness unrewarding at best.

## A Search for More Effective Methods of Intervention

During the 1980s, several of us in the statutory and voluntary sectors sought to find ways to remedy this unsatisfactory situation. After considerable experience of working with those whose lives had been affected by schizophrenia, it seemed to us that their valuable expertize was being wasted. Sufferers regularly commented that no-one asked them about their illness, nor about their ways of coping with it, even when they were in hospital. Families reported a similar indifference to their own experiences; they were no longer overtly blamed for causing this illness in their relative, as happened in the 1960s and 1970s, but they were still, as often as not, virtually ignored; this, despite the fact that many were expected to get on and support a vulnerable sufferer in the community. It seemed again and again that sufferers and carers had to rely on each other for survival, often without any real information about the illness which was causing so much havoc in their lives. Indeed, the President of the National Schizophrenia Fellowship, Professor John Wing, has marvelled at the way so many families do, nevertheless, cope:

> 'It is extraordinary that so many relatives do manage to find a way of living with schizophrenia that provides the patient with a supportive and non-threatening home'[5]

Of necessity, sufferers and carers have learnt the hard way and these survivors have built up an invaluable expertize that remains a largely untapped resource.

## A Knowledge Base

It seemed to us that the basic and important features of this type of illness were being overlooked or ignored. For example, I have found the most striking thing about schizophrenia to be the similarity of the experiences of those trying to cope with it. Repeatedly, on my first meeting with a recovered sufferer or with a carer, I am greeted with 'you won't believe this, but...' However, I find myself listening to a remarkably familiar story unfolding itself once more. I have been hearing it now for the best part of twenty years! This similarity of experience applies both to the interpretation many sufferers put on their nightmare experiences (demonstrating the brain's determined efforts to make sense of these experiences in a relevant and familiar context) and also to the difficulties that families have to face in their efforts to obtain help for a loved one.

My colleagues and I felt we could build up a knowledge-base from the experience of the real experts – sufferers and their relatives – which would help to identify needs. This proved to be the case and it has been achieved by the nurturing of a partnership between clients and service providers. This partnership has led to a humbling appreciation of what it really means to experience the symptoms of this illness and to have to cope with one's vulnerability in a society which shuns the very word 'schizophrenia'. Similarly, it has revealed the nature of a seeming obstacle race of peculiarly irrelevant and avoidable hazards facing anyone trying to support a sufferer in the community.

From these beginnings, it has not been too difficult to identify the real needs of those affected by a schizophrenic illness and to go on to develop ways of meeting some of these needs on a day-to-day basis. Some of the sufferers, carers and service providers involved in this partnership have contributed to later chapters in this book and hope that their experiences, ideas and comments will prove useful and, better still, perhaps stimulate ideas for change.

## A Need for Change

There is widespread dissatisfaction with society's present handling of severe mental illness. As we approach the final stages of the closing of the old mental hospitals, there is increasing concern over the evidence of neglect in the community, with psychotic individuals representing sizeable proportions of prison populations and of those living on the streets. This concern has escalated during 1993 as a result of a series of disasters reported by the media. These testify to the failure of community care, so far, to protect some of the most seriously mentally ill as well as the unfortunate members of the public who have suffered because of this. Stephen, who has survived 'the system' and shows every sign of thriving in the community, has made this wry observation on the changes taking place:

> EMPTY WARD
> In the sun drenched empty ward,
> There is a chair,
> Sat on and slept-in once,
> Because it was there,
> The whole ethos of care.
> The staff looked on,
> Like pupils watching the master,
> What can we do to help?
> Sorting out practical problems,
> Where society failed.
> The bugs have gone,
> Unlike the patients,
> Who are there in spirit,
> Like the medicated sunlight,
> Injecting its way across,
> But now they're on the street,
> Getting under politicians' feet.

Much of the debate has focused on the lack of adequate funding and resources. Although little enough money is spent on mental illness, the incessant call for more resources may actually be little more than a red herring where schizophrenia is concerned. Indeed, few sufferers and carers believe that even a saturation of resources would do much to improve their lot and some of us who specialize in working with schizophrenia firmly believe that the suffering and waste could be dramatically reduced even without any extra funding. Much of the rest of this book will address this matter but it might be useful at this stage to take a brief look at a few examples of the sort of obstacles referred to above which owe less to a need for more resources than to unwise use of existing ones.

## Getting into the System

It can be amazingly difficult to obtain acknowledgement that someone who is obviously becoming mentally ill is in need of medical attention. Long delays in obtaining help when someone is developing a psychotic illness are common. This is not the case with any other type of illness. We all take it for granted that the earlier a diagnosis and treatment can be obtained for any symptoms we develop, the better. In fact, we are urged to seek medical help sooner rather than later in order to optimize our chances of successful treatment. However, serious mental illness is the exception to the rule. Dangerous and damaging delays often occur before help is forthcoming. The nature and extent of such delays have been recorded in The Northwick Park Study of First Schizophrenic Episodes.[6] This research revealed that even when sick individuals were exhibiting extremely bizarre and, in some cases, clearly dangerous behaviour, delays in obtaining help often lasted over a year. Furthermore, in ten per cent of all cases, at least nine prior contacts were made with at least one service before help was provided. In a similar vein, an unpublished survey involving 889 families in the National Schizophrenia Fellowship[7] revealed that 161 sufferers obtained no help for their first schizophrenic episode *until the police intervened.*

The most likely reason for these tragic delays lies in deep-seated ideas that what we call mental illness is in fact 'a troubled mind' which cannot be treated in the same way as a sick body. There is wide acceptance that doctors practising medicine should look after our physical health, but this does not so readily apply when it comes to our mental health; suddenly the doctors' medicine becomes a 'chemical straitjacket'. Claims that schizophrenia is a myth rather than a treatable illness flourished in the anti-psychiatry heydays of the 1960s and 1970s and still live on. Around the same time, civil liberty lobbyists started to play what was to become a leading role in this debate. All these factors have contributed to an ideology which focuses on the right of the individual to deny one's mental illness, rather than on the duty of society to provide treatment and care. All those working with psychotic illness now work in a climate so influenced by such ideas that some psychiatrists feel apologetic and ambivalent about practising medicine in an area where others claim to have a monopoly of the 'moral high ground'.

In short, several factors have led to delays in 'getting into the system', but they do not include a lack of resources. Indeed, these very same delays actually put enormous extra pressure on existing resources because they preclude any chance of damage limitation and can lead to dangerous crisis situations.

## Avoiding Relapse

After a diagnosis and treatment have eventually been obtained, families and friends report the same sort of difficulties in trying to protect their loved ones from further breakdowns. This is frustrating when we know that each relapse brings a high risk of further damage. We have learned enough about this illness over recent years to make preventive care achievable. For example, we now know that when sufferers start to relapse there is a short time in which they recognize that this is happening and will accept help. Once this period has elapsed, the psychosis returns and our opportunity to prevent a breakdown is gone. Too often, by the time help is to hand, it is too late. The resulting delays and traumatic crises which inevitably arise only serve to put continued and avoidable pressure on scarce resources while incurring the risk of further damage to the sufferers themselves.

## Achieving a Quality of Life Compatible with Staying Well

Perhaps the most common and longstanding complaint from both carers and sufferers is about the dearth of available information about schizophrenia. It makes no sense at all for those most affected by this illness to be kept ignorant about what is happening to them. If individuals are to take responsibility for their own health, as encouraged in the present government's document Health of the Nation,[8] then they need to understand the nature of their illness. If, however, they are too handicapped to cope themselves, then those caring for them need to understand the nature of the illness and ways of coping with it. Both parties regularly report a lack of accessible knowledge about the illness and about the practical issues which contribute to survival in the community. These latter include basic components of everyday living such as welfare benefits, day-care facilities, sheltered housing, ongoing professional support and opportunities for peer contact. We are talking here about access to existing resources rather than about an absence of resources.

## Denial

We may add to this brief summary of some of the flaws in the present system an unspoken denial which really amounts to a conspiracy of silence about the whole subject of schizophrenia. This promotes widespread fear, ignorance and gross misunderstandings about the illness as well as increasing the stigma associated with it. Can there be any worse fate than to suffer from a diagnosis that no-one will talk about?

Fears of labelling which have led to the devaluing of a diagnosis of mental illness have actually worsened rather than improved the situation. On one hand, new sufferers are deprived of an early diagnosis (with its precious bonus of prompt treatment) and on the other, those who have to live with schizophrenia are either left ignorant of their diagnosis or feel compelled to pretend they do not have it. No wonder so many angrily deny their seemingly unmentionable illness and a need for any treatment! Some of us are old enough to remember a similar situation with cancer, another very common condition. Eventually, reason prevailed and we were all given the chance to learn about this dreaded group of diseases and to realize that cancer can and does happen to anybody, even to public idols. More important, we learned that there could be life after cancer if a positive approach is taken. This applies to schizophrenia too and, by denying its existence, we expose each new generation of sufferers to delayed treatment and, if their sickness persists, to 'third-class citizen' status.

These, then, are the sort of problems that need addressing while we wait for further funding. At the present time, we are wasting and under-using some existing resources while putting an impossible burden on others. In particular, the prevalent 'let's wait and see' approach actually provokes crisis situations which block our declining supply of 'acute beds', possibly our most precious and scarce resource. This in turn absorbs much of the skilled time of doctors and nurses out in the community chasing up available beds for urgent admissions while crisis situations increasingly turn into disasters.

## A Practical Guide

This book is about the experiences and needs of those who have to cope with a schizophrenic illness. It is not about the possible origins of schizophrenia, nor disputes over its definition, nor the political and ideological arguments surrounding it and which I have covered in some detail in a previous book.[9] It is about listening to and learning from sufferers and their relatives and finding ways to help them. It starts from the World Health Organization's conclusion in 1992 that:

> 'schizophrenic illnesses are ubiquitous, appear with similar incidence in different cultures and have clinical features that are more remarkable by their similarity across cultures than their difference'[10]

## CHAPTER 2

# What Happens to Sufferers

There tends to be some confusion about the use of the terms 'acute' and 'chronic' in schizophrenia. Much of this is due to the usual practice of describing any long-term condition as chronic. It is not helpful if we do this with schizophrenia because many sufferers remain well for long periods, experiencing perhaps just one or two relapses after their first schizophrenic episode. For this reason, we usually refer to their illness as 'acute' schizophrenia and describe the more handicapping and permanent form of the illness as 'chronic' schizophrenia. The latter is mainly characterized by an undermining lethargy, a lack of 'get up and go', a flatness of emotion, and an inability to initiate and maintain a casual conversation. Such symptoms are described as 'negative' because they take something away from the original personality. Meanwhile, the word 'positive' is used to indicate symptoms that add something new to the individual's experience, however bizarre and unwelcome. Let's take a closer look at these type of experiences.

## Some 'Positive' Symptoms

An acute schizophrenic episode may include three main types of experiences and the technical terms used to describe these are *altered perception, delusional thinking* and *an abnormal thought structure*. Let's take a look at some examples of each of these.

### Altered Perception

This can affect all of the five senses we use to interpret the world around us and if this happens then our rapport with our environment is threatened; everything we have learned to take for granted is undermined. It is as if our senses are playing tricks on us. The senses of vision, hearing, smell, touch and taste may all be distorted.

What does this mean to the individual? It can mean that colours may seem too bright or too dull or that people and objects may look odd, change shape or become grotesque in appearance. Music and other sounds may seem shrill and too high pitched to sensitive ears and every sound in the background may become as noisy as those close at hand. The sense of smell may become acutely sensitive; one result of this can be to become unusually aware of normal body odour in oneself and others. Everyday things may take on an unnaturally sweet and exotic fragrance or equally well they may give off a foul and rotting stench. An object, such as a table which should be flat and hard may feel three-dimensional and furry. Food and drink may taste bitter or 'coppery'.

Some of these experiences are examples of acutely heightened sensitivity, and loss of an innate ability to 'select out' unimportant and irrelevant messages. What can this mean to the sufferer? Ralph has described this as 'being bombarded with stimuli, rather like a radio receiving half a dozen stations at once'. Sally has written:

> 'There was a period when I was afraid to look in the dressing-table mirror because of the large purple vein which I could plainly see running down the side of my nose. It had been there for at least three days, I was convinced, and was still obvious even when I checked in the bathroom mirror. The sight of that awful worm-like shape made me fear that I might be beginning yet another breakdown.

> There were also nightmarish visions of people I thought I saw looking in the window of my basement flat; sometimes these had half a face or were grotesquely distorted in other ways. Besides this, even before my illness, I had had a horror of birds, so that I was doubly affected by what I perceived to be the gigantic size of the pigeons which congregated in the garden just outside my flat. All these things were weirdly menacing, particularly as there was no colour in what I thought I saw – everything was either grey or black or white.

> When I am in a breakdown my sense of smell is hypersensitive. I am convinced that my body odour is foul and that grease and dirt are oozing from my pores. As well as this, my surroundings appear to be intolerably grimy. At other times, I am bombarded by peremptory voices (sometimes obeyed) ordering me to injure myself. Then again, I am sure I can hear people in the next room plotting against me. During these bouts I sometimes convinced myself that if I put my head

under cold water I would be able to get rid of the voices, and on occasions this did in fact work.

During these distorted states it seemed to me that everyone — particularly my own family — was against me and kept committing me to hospital just to get rid of me. In this state I felt reluctant to talk about these things for fear of being thought mad. Therefore for a long while I kept everything hidden. Eventually, however, I did come to trust those who were trying to help me and so I arrived at a better understanding of my illness.'

Some examples of altered perception, such as smells and sounds which cannot be explained, are hallucinatory experiences and the best known of these are the voices which are a common feature of a schizophrenic illness. It is important to note that these are actually *heard* rather than imagined but we don't yet understand the mechanics of this phenomenon. Such voices may talk about the individual in the 'third-person', carrying on an unwelcome commentary on his or her actions such as, 'Look at her now, she's picking up the phone!' This must be acutely frustrating and tiring as well as disturbing. Carol North, a practising psychiatrist in the USA, has written a dramatic account of day-to-day life with her voices during the years she suffered with an acute schizophrenic illness.[1]

Another type of voice may also talk about the individual in the third-person but be perceived as belonging to a loved one, or someone else who *matters*, thus causing deep unhappiness and feelings of betrayal if their comments are hostile. For Pat, this meant hearing her father's voice plotting to kill her night after night because she had apparently fatally harmed her mother in some way. How could she cope with such a nightmare? She did not know she was ill and knew nothing of a common experience called 'hearing voices'. She did try to challenge her parents several times, telling them pointedly 'I know what's happening' but they protested that they did not understand what she was saying...

The third type of voice commonly experienced, and which Sally has mentioned, is the one that shouts insults or instructions to the individual, sometimes urging self-damage or damage to others. Jonathan is one of five sufferers I have known who have jumped from a window and permanently damaged themselves, not because they wanted to push the 'self-destruct' button but through fear of defying these overpowering voices telling them to jump at the point of breakdown. Jonathan explains, almost apologetically, 'I couldn't listen to them any longer'. It is difficult to imagine the extent of a terror that is greater than the prospect of wilfully damaging yourself in this way. Sufferers stress, when recovered, that the voices become so real and compelling that everything else pales into insignificance.

Less common are the visionary hallucinations which some individuals experience, perhaps seeing a 'ghost' (who may take up residence!) or perhaps a sudden flashing of lights, or a brilliant aura or similar phenomenon. For some individuals, this may be a encouraging confirmation of a reassuring religious belief. But for Jean, a middle-aged housewife and mother, just one such experience led to a delusion that she had been singled out for a 'visitation'. She believed that she faced 'eternal hell and damnation' because she had had two wartime affairs before meeting her husband. For many years the distorted feelings of guilt, so common in schizophrenia, had been escalated by this hallucinatory experience and tormented her whenever she was particularly vulnerable.

These, then, are some of the more usual type of hallucinations experienced in schizophrenia. Perhaps we should not be surprised that many of the delusional ideas, another common feature of this type of illness, seem frequently to be related to them. We have seen instances of this with Pat and Jean. A more typical example of a connection between the two types of symptoms can be seen when individuals, already feeling inexplicably ill, find their food and drink tasting bitter or coppery and become convinced they are being systematically poisoned; a not unreasonable conclusion in the circumstances.

## Delusional Ideas

These may be described as fixations which are impervious to reason. It can be a confounding experience to attempt to persuade someone who has such a fixation that there is no logical basis to this; it is also a waste of time.

Perhaps the most common delusional ideas in this illness are those of paranoia. Most of us have had persecutionary ideas at some time in our day-to-day lives but there is a significant difference between these and the paranoia experienced in a psychotic illness. Here the persecutionary ideas come *from within*. They are not an over-sensitive reaction to an outside stimulus such as the feeling we may experience if we approach a group of people who burst out laughing as we hurry by. In a psychotic illness, the paranoia is experienced in the absence of such normal stimuli. For example, Pat's paranoia about her father was based entirely on hearing a voice which was part of her illness. His behaviour towards her continued to be as loving as it had been previously when they had always enjoyed a good, close relationship. In fact, the paranoia of a schizophrenic illness almost invariably focuses initially on those who matter most to the individual, with potentially devastating results for all concerned, unless they are made aware of this.

Grandiose ideas frequently feature in delusional thinking. Sufferers may believe they are Joan of Arc, or some other famous or notorious character. Equally, they may believe that they can control the minds, thoughts and speech of others or even that they are all powerful and can change the course of history. More disturbingly, they can be tormented with ideas that they are responsible for all the evil in the world and, more specifically, for the latest disaster reported in the media. Tina, whose breakdown coincided with the Falklands War, believed herself to have been responsible for this. She was never able to explain how this could be so but she *just knew* she had brought about the deaths and suffering resulting from these hostilities. Can we start to imagine the pain and suffering that such a conviction could cause a previously carefree and confident eighteen-year-old?

The other side of the coin of being able to control the minds and read the thoughts of others is to believe that the reverse may be true. For some sufferers this brings a conviction that their thoughts are being broadcast for all to hear; an awesome prospect. Tony used to avoid any confined space such as a bus or a surgery waiting room, as he could not risk being trapped amongst a group of people who were being entertained to a revelation of all his innermost thoughts. There was no persuading him otherwise because, as he patiently explained, he could tell by looking at other people's faces that this was happening.

*Ideas of reference* often feature in a delusional nightmare. Sufferers may believe that everything going on around them refers to them. Any physical movement such as the tapping of a foot or the rubbing of a nose can be a sign, a message about themselves, which everyone else understands. Similarly, innocent words can be interpreted as *double talk* which usually involves disparaging remarks about the individual.

More typically, the radio and television can become 'no go' areas for sufferers affected by ideas of reference because everything happening on them appears to be addressed at themselves. They talk of switching on the television only to see and hear the newsreader referring to them and using their name. I once sat with a middle-aged man at the point of breakdown, who shouted abuse at the television screen whilst intermittently pointing out to me that the programme was relaying the details of his life for all to hear. All I could see on the screen were dozens of horses against a background of shouting and gunfire in a very noisy Western. After a while he could take no more of this extraordinary experience and angrily turned the set off, amazed that I would not acknowledge what was happening.

Delusional ideas about sex also feature in this illness and sometimes these result in confusion about one's own sexual identity. I have come across several heterosexual men who have tormented themselves in their belief that they had suddenly become homosexual ('tormented' because this was quite unacceptable to them precisely because it was not true). Bernard has been experiencing this for some time now. He has no intention of testing out his newly assumed and unwelcome homosexuality but is certain that it is recorded in some way on his face for all to see. He complains every time he goes out of muttered comments of recognition by all those he meets or passes in the street; 'they think I don't hear them', he complains sadly. He is impervious to suggestions that there would seem to be no reasonable explanation for this hostility.

Perhaps more troublesome is the confusion over sexual boundaries that occur in some cases; male sufferers may see their mother – sometimes the only woman they have any daily contact with – as an appropriate subject for their sexual advances. Rather differently, sufferers may accuse a parent of having sexual designs on them. These ideas can cause severe embarrassment and hurt for both parties. Similarly, it is not unknown for female sufferers to believe they are pregnant for years on end or to report having had sexual intercourse on a closely supervised ward each night. Fortunately, perhaps, although such delusional ideas can be very pervasive, they do not affect the majority of sufferers.

A preoccupation with religious ideas is a very common feature of schizophrenia and where these are associated with existing feelings of guilt then sufferers may believe they have been singled out for damnation as happened in Jean's case. This sort of experience can be very real for the individual, so much so that some young people I have known have spent hours on end scouring the Bible for examples of forgiveness and mercy which might bear good tidings for them. Such is the potential torment of delusional thinking.

Delusions about the body are also common and these may take several forms, from the conviction that one's body has been invaded by another being, spiritual or otherwise, through to beliefs that one's brain or muscles are melting or wasting away.

When breaking down, many sufferers believe that they are terminally ill or have any number of grave physical ailments. Colin was admitted to hospital at 19 years of age and sent on his way a few weeks later with no diagnosis other than 'hypochondria'. His fears of impending death having faded in the safety of a hospital ward, his mental illness remained undetected for a further two years before he suffered a now inevitable and severe breakdown. Similarly, John was investigated for all sorts of unconfirmed physical problems during the time he was developing a schizophrenic illness and mental illness was not recognised as the underlying cause. Several years later, as we shall see, this all happened again, with renewed complaints of a series of physical problems again heralding a schizophrenic breakdown.

Significantly, these real concerns in some sufferers about their health never include consideration of the possibility that they might have a *mental* illness, despite any previous history of this. Indeed, it would seem that the core delusion in schizophrenia is a fixation that one has no such condition! Certainly, this frequently embedded delusion puts sufferers of this illness more at risk than those of any other.

## Abnormal Thought Structure

Abnormal thought structure can affect different individuals in different ways. It can result in one's thoughts seeming to take on a life of their own, flitting frantically from subject to subject or, alternatively, focusing on one idea to the exclusion of all else. Such experiences might well explain why those sufferers so affected are sure that their minds are being controlled by outside forces.

The individual may find his attention focused indefinitely on some innocuous object for no apparent reason and this *capture of attention* may well explain another phenomenon in this illness: *heightened significance*, in which all sorts of things take on a special meaning. This may apply to a colour (often yellow, I'm told), to a word, to an object, to a person or other living creature, to a time or to a happening. Each and everything which attracts the individual's attention assumes importance and a special meaning. Often, a number plate is mentioned – the one on the rear of the car in front – as having a special meaning immediately understood by the sufferer. Nigel claimed that he at last understood that there was a sinister plot to kill him when a colleague gave him a lift and he noted the significance of the number-plate ahead of them at the traffic lights. Now well again, he is unable to explain this further.

Similarly, it is quite common for sufferers to believe that answers to the greater mysteries of life have been revealed to them as in an inspiration. One has explained:

> 'I was suddenly confronted with an overwhelming conviction that I had discovered the secrets of the universe, which were being rapidly made plain with incredible lucidity ... I had no sense or doubt or the awareness of the possibility of doubt'[2]

For some, these sorts of experiences can be fascinating and stimulating. This is not the case, however, with a similar type of symptom described as an *intrusive thought*. These thoughts can be particularly cruel; they could better be described as unwanted, sometimes obscene, thoughts which persistently absorb the individual's attention. Matthew is a sensitive young man, well liked by his peers, and is particularly good with children. Keen to work with them one day, he was plagued for several years by ideas that he should sexually assault a child. For some months before these thoughts eventually faded, Matthew refused to go outside of his home because he was frightened that he might really do something so abhorrent to him. Another young man I know is particularly loving towards animals and he is plagued by ideas that he must viciously hurt them. Talking about this has helped to allay his fears but for a long time he felt unable to do this in case others would osctracize him for such seemingly 'wicked thoughts'. Significantly, intrusive thoughts frequently seem to have the same characteristic as paranoid ideas in that they tend to focus in on subjects particularly dear to the sufferer.

Perhaps it is predictable that not only do unwanted thoughts intrude into one's consciousness but other thoughts appear to be snatched away, with the mind suddenly blocking and becoming completely blank. This happens at any time in any situation; not just during an exam or in the middle of giving a speech as might happen to any of us. At best, sufferers find it frustrating and, at worst, very embarrassing. It also confirms ideas that an outside force is governing one's mind, and, clearly, this can be very frightening.

*Comment*

These, then, are some of the more usual 'positive symptoms' which may occur in an acute schizophrenic breakdown and which are often responsive to the anti-psychotic drugs discovered in the early 1950s, bringing about a revolution in the treatment of this type of illness. Clearly, no episode will involve all these symptoms although some sufferers do in fact experience all or most over the course of several breakdowns. It is more usual, however, for each individual's illness to follow a similar pattern involving several repeating symptoms rather than covering the whole spectrum. In particular, if paranoia is a dominant feature in a first breakdown, then it is likely to be so in any further episode.

Perhaps it would be useful at this point to fit these bizarre experiences into a background which gives a more complete picture of the sufferer's psychotic nightmare. Many a schizophrenic episode starts abruptly with a feeling that *something awful has happened.* Some individuals describe it as though 'a switch of doom and gloom' has been turned on. Suddenly they are alienated from all around them and convinced that everyone knows what is wrong except for themselves. They are sure they must have done something dreadful; they become anxious and excessively self-conscious. In this illness, self-consciousness can mean being so uncomfortably aware of yourself that you have no time to notice what is happening around you; you cannot concentrate on what others are saying or doing. It can mean visibly trembling with embarrassment if someone's attention focuses on you. One sufferer has described this as feeling like 'a shining beacon', for all to see.

Bearing in mind the experiences that sufferers may fall victim to, it is not really surprising that some become clinically depressed nor that many feel worthless and despicable and may refer to themselves as 'evil' while they are ill.

Before finishing with a brief discussion on the 'negative' symptoms of the illness, it might be useful to take a look at a few phenonemons which may feature in both the acute and chronic forms of schizophrenia.

## Eye Contact

It is not uncommon for a sufferer's medical notes to comment 'better eye contact today'. Some sufferers find it almost impossible to look into another person's eyes when they are not well; they will constantly look down whilst speaking or listening to others. Unfortunately, this can be seen as anti-social and Clive was actually told by a mental health professional on one occasion, 'please look at me when I'm talking to you!' This young man explains that he doesn't expose his face to the other person's eyes when he is experiencing his main symptom: a delusion that his face muscles are distorting and making him look grotesque.

## Turning Day into Night

An unwelcome and particularly anti-social feature of schizophrenia can be the upturning of the body's 24-hour clock. This can make life difficult for everyone in the household as the sufferer tends to 'come to life' late in the evening, eventually retiring to bed just before most of the rest of the world rises. This is so real that when Sue asked me to call for her and wake her up one morning so that she didn't miss a group outing, she managed to get herself up and join us, only to fall asleep one hour later standing in the middle of a crowded store!

## An Eating Disorder

For some sufferers, there seems to be a strong element of eating disorder in their illness. It can be an extraordinary experience to visit a hospital ward at meal-times and to witness some patients wolfing down their food, particularly stodgy 'junk food'. It is as if they are starving animals on the rampage. There is no regard for the niceties of table manners or the needs of others. Individuals affected in this way have reported real embarrassment at their own behaviour when they can't deal with their craving for this sort of food in any other way. The significance of this quite common phenomenon has tended to be overlooked because it has been assumed that the appetite-stimulating component in the anti-psychotic drugs is responsible for this abnormal eating behaviour. This cannot be the case as (a) families so often report this as one of the first signs that something is wrong with their relative (long before treatment is available) and (b) many sufferers on these drugs have no such problem.

## Water Intoxication Syndrome

Similarly, another common feature in a psychotic illness is a constant thirst (also observed in severely hyperactive children). In some sufferers this escalates to dangerous levels when they are not at all well. Unless restrained, they may literally pour pints of water or milk down their throats, in what seems like a matter of minutes. A recent hospital death[3] may have promoted new interest in this largely ignored phenomenon.

## 'Negative' Symptoms

This very different type of symptom is, of course, the main feature of the chronic form of the illness. Nevertheless, it is important to note that some 'negative' symptoms may also feature in an acute breakdown and in its immediate aftermath. It is when the symptoms persist that they are likely to represent the more disabling condition which may be irreversible. Seemingly unresponsive to the main medication used for a schizophrenic illness, there is growing evidence that recently released drugs may have more effect on the 'negative' symptoms of this illness.

The persistence of 'negative' symptoms can alter the personality to the point where sufferers can become a shadow of their original selves. In very severe cases, families can feel that they have lost their loved one, who may seem almost a stranger because so much has been lost from the original familiar personality. The most significant change in this respect may be a seeming inability to experience and, certainly, to express emotion. Sufferers themselves may complain of an overwhelming flatness and the absence of feelings such as those of excitement, of anticipation or of elation. For them, every day is the same. Even food may lose its interest and be eaten for the sake of it and not because of feelings of hunger.

Can we begin to imagine what it would be like to experience none of the ups and downs which are so much part of our daily lives; to lose the occasional thrill of anticipation and excitement, to have no interest in what tomorrow may bring? No wonder these frequently young men and women complain that they are bored and show little interest in doing anything about it.

The core of this chronic form of the illness is a lack of motivation and this is aggravated by an almost overwhelming lethargy which is very real and can be likened to the feeling some of us experience after a heavy bout of influenza. The chronic sufferer is unlikely to want to mix socially, initially anyway, as there is a marked inability to make conversation, particularly the sort we describe as 'small-talk' and which we use so much in our everyday dealings with the rest of the world. If we add to this *poverty of speech* a lack of staying power, due in part to an inability to concentrate on even popular escapist pleasures such as reading, listening to radio and watching television, then we begin to understand why we have to work so hard to persuade many of these individuals to do more than just sit or lie down for hours on end, staring into space.

The chronic form of schizophrenic illness is often visibly recognizable by those who have seen it before but it is difficult to explain exactly why this is. Some chronic sufferers have a dishevelled, neglected appearance, due to a pronounced disinterest in themselves and their hygiene, but they often also look alienated and unwell, with an unnatural pallor. More specifically, there is often a jerky gait, aggravated by an impression of limp and floppy muscles. The undermining physical exhaustion can almost be felt by the onlooker, together with a core, disabling, lack of motivation. Because the illness is more visible, chronic sufferers are less likely than those recovering from an acute breakdown to be accused of malingering. It is an irony that some of the most disabled of them are also less likely to take the trouble to claim their rights.

## In Conclusion

These, then are some of the experiences of schizophrenia. We could be forgiven for believing that the 'positive' and 'negative' symptoms represent two different illnesses. If this is so, they are nevertheless interrelated, as the latter symptoms can be observed in the immediate aftermath of an acute episode and, similarly, sufferers with the chronic form of the schizophrenia are still prone to relapse into acute breakdowns.

Due to the confusion when we refer to the 'acute' or 'chronic' form of the illness, it may be far more helpful to use Dr Tim Crow's classification of schizophrenia[4] in which he refers to the Type I and Type II syndromes. The Type I syndrome covers the 'positive' symptoms, which usually respond well to medication, with no expectation of intellectual impairment or irreversible damage. The Type II syndrome covers the 'negative' symptoms, with a poor response to medication, with possible intellectual impairment and a perhaps irreversible condition. The advantage of this classification is that it precludes the use of the word 'chronic' to describe the illness of a sufferer who may have just two or three acute episodes in a lifetime and clarifies which type of illness we are talking about.

CHAPTER 3

# What Happens to Families

Having looked at the potential inner world of the sufferer, it is worth noting that the more harrowing this becomes, the less the outside world can intrude upon the individual; the horrors of an untreated psychosis are as terrifying and all-absorbing in the comforts of a palace as they are in the privations of a hovel. For carers it could not be more different; when someone they love develops a schizophrenic illness, they become entirely dependent upon the outside world. They are frighteningly powerless to help themselves without the intervention of others. Only the appropriate diagnosis and treatment can free them from a psychotic nightmare.

How do families fare when they seek this help and intervention? Too often they find themselves struggling in their own nightmare; a nightmare in which their relative turns into a stranger in front of their eyes while the rest of the world seems to deny that there is anything wrong.

How can this happen? It happens for the sort of reasons we discussed in the first chapter. It happens because ignorance about schizophrenia means that most of us know nothing about it unless we become involved with it. It happens because of a 'let's wait and see' approach amongst those who do know about it, which serves to deny the unwelcome prospect of a serious illness in a hitherto healthy young person. It happens because the whole system is geared to react to crisis rather than towards prevention. It happens because the rest of the world has gone mad, or so it sometimes seems to those trying to obtain acknowledgement that a loved one is sick and in need of help!

## How it all starts

Consider what happened to one family living in the West country, when they sought help. Malcolm, a sociable and gifted boy of sixteen years, entered the sixth form to study for his 'A' levels in the autumn of 1985. Shortly afterwards his parents became worried because he was suddenly finding fault with everyone and his family and could do nothing right. After a while, he refused to have anything to do with his close friends and he started finding excuses to avoid going to school.

Christmas was a difficult time with the parents unable to find out what was the matter with their eldest child. When the holiday was over, Malcolm refused to go back to school. He spent the daytime lying on his bed and prowled around the house most of the night. He wouldn't eat with the rest of the family and made dreadful scenes if they sat down to watch television because it was 'too noisy'. He would then go to his bedroom and play a couple of tapes over and over again at full volume. His two small brothers, still at primary school, were becoming nervous and edgy in his company. When his father decided to seek help from the family's GP, she was sympathetic and promised to have a careful look at Malcolm when he next came to the surgery.

## Acknowledgement

Two months later, the doctor decided that Malcolm was depressed and she persuaded him to see a psychiatrist, who eventually admitted the boy to a psychiatric unit for assessment shortly before his seventeenth birthday. Four weeks later he was discharged, seemingly without having received any treatment. The doctor met once with the parents, during a crowded ward round with Malcolm present, and told them that there was nothing to worry about; nothing that was unusual in adolescence. He suggested that they and Malcolm should attend for family therapy sessions with a nurse and a social worker.

Malcolm ran out of the first session and never turned up for family therapy again. The parents came away depressed and frustrated after each session. They picked up messages that they were 'too demanding' and also 'under-rating Malcolm's need for independence at this time'. They explained that, on the contrary, they were actually concerned that he was becoming more and more *dependent* upon his mother and refusing to leave the house. They felt they were not being heard. Similarly, when they mentioned the sort of things which were happening at home every day, which they assumed would demonstrate how difficult life was becoming for the whole family, the therapists made no comment. Malcolm's mother and father did not feel they were being listened to; they were still alone with their overwhelming problems. After seven weeks, the therapists discontinued the sessions.

## An Ongoing Nightmare

During the autumn of 1986, Malcolm's behaviour was becoming stranger all the time. Most of the time he would lie on his bed unless he and his mother were alone in the house, when he would come down and follow her everywhere. His unprovoked outbursts when other members of the family were at home were no longer confined to verbal aggression; on several occasions he threw crockery across the kitchen, once just missing his mother's face. Nevertheless, he became increasingly clinging towards her and intensely jealous of any attention she gave anyone else. She, in turn, found him distant and morose, but his young brothers were now very wary of him. It seemed as if the whole family were walking a tightrope, with no way of controlling what was happening to them. Meanwhile Malcolm rarely left the house and he refused to go to his outpatient appointments, as well as carefully avoiding his GP.

A year or so after this all began, Malcolm's mother told the GP she could not cope much longer. Her eldest son was obviously deeply unhappy, but so angry that they all found his behaviour very threatening. To her despair, the GP replied that she could do nothing further as Malcolm refused to keep his outpatient appointments or to go to her surgery. That, it seemed, was the end of the matter.

One evening three months later, when his father was working late, Malcolm threatened his mother, holding a bread knife to her throat. His brothers watched, screaming with fear. After a night of trauma, Malcolm was persuaded next day by a doctor and a social worker to go back into hospital, on a voluntary basis. When he discharged himself nine days later, the distraught parents pleaded for more help and were told that Malcolm was 'not sectionable' now he had had sanctuary and medication which had calmed him, but they would keep a bed open for him if he would accept this. If pigs could fly, they thought...

## Bad Not Mad

By April 1987, life had become a nightmare. Teachers were expressing concern about the welfare and progress of the two younger boys. Meanwhile, the parents noted that health professionals were talking of *bad behaviour* rather than *illness* when they referred to Malcolm and even asking the parents why they were prepared to put up with this?

In July 1987, Malcolm's father managed to arrange a further outpatient appointment for his son but when the time came to set out for the clinic, Malcolm physically attacked his mother when she tried to persuade him to come out of his bedroom. In tears, she took herself and her blackened eye round to the GP's surgery, begging for help. The GP sympathized and then reiterated what others had said before her, 'You don't have to put up with this sort of behaviour, you know!'

## Family Breakdown

That evening, the parents decided they had no choice; if the rest of the family was to survive, then Malcolm must go. The next morning they asked social workers to help them find digs for their son. This was the most painful moment of their lives; one they will never forgive.

Over the next twenty months, Malcolm's parents watched a steady deterioration in him; his face became haggard, his eyes glazed and he showed no interest in his appearance or hygiene. Several times the police had to intervene to protect the rest of the family when he visited home and became threatening or actually attacked his mother. The parents noted that the police seemed to recognize the real nature of the family's plight and agreed that the young man was very sick, while health professionals categorically denied this. Meanwhile, this weary and depressed mother spent much of her time during those traumatic months trekking the streets to find her son new accommodation after failing to pacify one outraged landlady after another.

One night in August 1989, Malcolm was discovered trying to set light to his latest lodgings. He was apprehended just in time to prevent a tragedy. He was at last formally admitted to hospital under section and given appropriate treatment and care for his schizophrenic illness. Malcolm was very damaged by this time; the violence provoked by his untreated terrors soon disappeared but – four years later – he is still not well enough to live outside of hospital. The family are reunited in the sense that he occasionally goes home for weekend visits. However, his mother cannot envisage a time when they could welcome him home permanently; her memories of violence in the sanctuary of her home are still vivid, together with the nightmare of never knowing what will happen next.

## Comment

When this case was discussed at a study day for mental health workers, they were at a loss to suggest what else these parents could have done to obtain the help that Malcolm needed. They were, however, able to pinpoint at least several occasions when professionals could have intervened positively and rescued the family. We will take a further look at their role later, but, meanwhile, what do you think you might have wanted to do if you had been involved with this case?

This sad saga illustrates the way in which families are totally dependent on others to rescue them. Many wait far too long for any such help and all but a very few fortunate families experience prolonged delays before they obtain acknowledgement of a developing schizophrenic illness and effective help from professionals.

## A 'Let's Wait and See' Policy

I have described elsewhere[1] how the endless delays feel for the carers and for the sufferer with a 'blow-by-blow' account of a typical family's experience. In this particular case, the parents are advised by doctors not to fuss; the son is encouraged by professionals to go off to college and stand on his own two feet. He does just that, despite an almost overwhelming need to be with his mother. She is powerless to stop him, although all her instincts tell her he should not go away on his own; powerless because she and her husband can get no confirmation from 'the experts' that their son is sick and needing help.

More often than not, young people who may be developing schizophrenia are encouraged to get on with their lives, as though nothing were wrong, even when this means their leaving the security and shelter of their home. They gladly take such advice from a doctor or other health professional who is reassuring them that they are just fine and need to become independent. They take this sort of advice because they so need to believe that this is true.

Those who go away to college will almost certainly find themselves living and studying amongst strangers. Their peers will probably label them 'odd', or 'a loner', and forget about them. Their tutors will be lucky if they set eyes on them. When they eventually break down in this lonely world which they have moved into, their illness may well be put down to the strain of studying.

Other similarly vulnerable young people, sometimes less academically inclined, may decide they'd find peace and sanctuary abroad and again may be encouraged to go ahead with such plans. I have worked with young sufferers who have been deported and sent home from distant countries following their breakdown. A few have found themselves in potentially dangerous situations in quite hostile circumstances and we can only be thankful they found their way home, albeit by deportation. Just how many parents would prescribe this sort of experience for their healthy teenage sons and daughters, let alone one who is sick and vulnerable?

## A 'de-skilling' Process

It is worrying that parents are actually persuaded to go along with ideas which their instincts tell them are wrong. This happens when those who should know all about the potential dangers – professionals who work with mental illness – won't confirm parents' conviction that their child has become vulnerable and sick. Instead, the parents are allowed to believe that they are to blame in some way; they may have been over-protective or too loath to let this offspring 'fly the nest'. Few well-meaning parents want to make these sort of mistakes; they are already asking themselves 'what have we done wrong?'. They feel guilty and perplexed and they listen to what the professionals have to say.

Thus, we can engage in the destructive process of stripping parents of their skills; skills which have probably served other offspring perfectly well. Owing to the widespread ignorance of schizophrenia, most parents have no real knowledge about this common and debilitating illness that we should expect to find in a significantly large minority of young people in the prime of life. If they did have such knowledge, distraught parents might challenge professionals who talk about a 'minor adolescent disturbance' and ask 'could this be schizophrenia?' and ask for reassurance that this is not the case before sanctioning a change of lifestyle which could expose the young person to unacceptable risks. As it is, confused and undermined, they listen to professionals specializing in such matters and reluctantly let them take responsibility for their child's future and safety because they seem to have no other option.

## Families in Turmoil

This, then, is how it all starts for many of those seeking help for a young person developing a schizophrenic illness. A year or two, sometimes more, may expire between the first alarm over a dramatic change in personality and the eventual breakdown that *does* demand acknowledgement. What happens to families during these long periods of denial and delay?

At best, they stay together, trying to cope with behaviour they cannot understand and trying to protect the sufferer from embarrassing situations.

The latter are particularly painful for brothers and sisters at an age where it is mandatory to 'fit' into the crowd, to be the same as your peers; not to have a brother who runs and hides as their friends come into the house or, worse, behaves very strangely in their company. They quickly learn to keep their friends away and often give their home a wide berth themselves rather than watch their parents' pain and apparent inability to help the son or daughter who has become a stranger in their midst. Some feel very angry about this seeming inadequacy; why don't Mum and Dad *do* something? Others share their parents' protective attitude towards the sick brother or sister, loyally defending this vulnerable family member. Most families eventually 'turn in on themselves', keeping a potentially critical world at bay and protecting the sufferer from a society which stigmatizes mental illness. It is an absurd irony that most families, and those in contact with them, define the cause of the problem as a serious mental illness long before mental health professionals confirm this.

## Life After Schizophrenia

If these are the sort of problems which beset families trying to obtain help for a relative developing a schizophrenic illness, do things improve for them once the sufferer's sickness has been acknowledged? It would be tempting to believe that most of their problems would be resolved at this point, but this is often not the case. First, families rarely obtain any helpful explanations about what has happened to them. Second, and more important, neither do they obtain adequate information on how to cope in the future. Medical advisers to the National Schizophrenia Fellowship (NSF) reported in *The Bulletin of the Royal College of Psychiatrists* in 1985 that:

> 'one of the chief problems mentioned by the relatives of people suffering from schizophrenia is the difficulty in obtaining factual and practical advice. Many have struggled on for years using trial and error methods'[2]

and a small survey in 1993, carried out by a local NSF group, confirmed feedback received from national organizations that this is indeed the common experience of carers.[3]

Amazingly, some families are not even told the diagnosis when this is eventually made, nor given any information about the treatment their relative is receiving. I know parents who have actually been told, in answer to their request for a diagnosis, 'well, he doesn't have schizophrenia' or 'we don't think she has schizophrenia'. This, it seems, has sufficed for a diagnosis and accompanying explanation. The patient has then been discharged after successful treatment with anti-psychotic medication and has been expected to persevere in taking medication for a non-existent illness. Not surprisingly, the inherent scepticsm sufferers have about their illness and any need for medication is only reinforced by this sort of evasive behaviour in those responsible for their medical care. For those who obtain neither a diagnosis, nor any information about what has happened, the future is bleak.

What about those who fare better than this? Once over the first shock (and it certainly comes as a shock to learn that a loved one has such an illness), carers always report feelings of relief that they have an explanation for what has happened to them and know the name and nature of the beast which is responsible for this. Now, they can at least approach organizations concerned with schizophrenia and also seek out literature on the illness. Many read up the subject, becoming conversant with up-to-date research and developing very real skills and expertise. The more fortunate are able to help their relative back to good health. Others are left struggling with the task of caring for damaged relatives who remain a shadow of their former self, never destined to achieve anything like their original potential. Most carers find themselves trying to cope with a situation somewhere between these two examples.

### An Ever Present Risk

It is important to remember – and this is where we came in – that all sufferers will still remain dependent, to a greater or lesser extent, on the intervention of others if they are not to be engulfed once more by a psychotic nightmare. Jan and her husband were delighted with their son's speedy recovery from his first schizophrenic episode, which started a year or so after leaving school. Gradually, he took up his old interests again and managed a part-time job as well. He was soon showing all his old potential and enjoying a near normal lifestyle and after two years his parents helped him to set up home on his own. A few months later, they became anxious again because their son was becoming hostile towards them and was starting to give up his newly revived interests.

### *Relapse*

When Jan approached her son's psychiatrist and told her 'something is wrong; he has done so well but something is going wrong again' she replied 'well, what do you expect with schizophrenia?'. Jan asked if he could have another outpatient appointment now instead of waiting two months for his next one? The doctor refused this request and when she eventually saw the young man she reduced his medication because he complained he felt too 'tired and dozy' to cope with his busy timetable (although he had given up his job and all of his hobbies again by then).

From that time on, things deteriorated fast and the young man became very ill again. He was particularly hostile towards his mother; his closest ally in the past. Jan and her husband begged for help from the hospital, from the psychiatrist, from the GP and from local social workers; all to no avail.

### A Love-hate Relationship

Eventually, when they pointed out to local professionals that life was becoming unbearable for the family, they were told that they were too possessive and demanding of their son and they were told to 'back off' and leave the caring to the mental health team. This was not an easy thing to do when they could find no evidence of any 'caring'. Moreover, how was Jan to 'pull back and stop interfering' when her son was phoning or visiting at least once a day to tell her, noisily and at great length, to get out of his life? Even as she wished herself a thousand miles away, so her sick son was finding excuses to make frequent contact with her, accusing her of interfering in his daily life. He was in fact using his mother as a lifeline, whilst persuading others that she, and not his illness, was the cause of his problems.

Jan and her husband did eventually leave the 'caring' to the mental health team; they had no choice because they couldn't get anyone to intervene and rescue their son from his illness. This caring was so inadequate that at one point, fifteen long months after Jan first sought help, her son realized himself that he was not coping and turned up at the hospital ward where he had been treated for his breakdown. He asked if he could have a meal and stay there for a few nights? He was sent away with 'this is not a hotel!'.

### Inevitable Breakdown

Eventually, one night several months later, the young man broke down and was taken to hospital. He was admitted on a voluntary basis because the psychiatrist did not want to spoil her relationship with him by forcing him into hospital. Now too ill to realize he needed help, her patient refused medication and would not stay in the hospital. He left three times during the next two weeks. Despite his distraught parents' continuous pleas, their son was not 'sectioned' and detained in hospital for urgently needed treatment until after the third time he went missing. On this occasion he eventually turned up at a police station in another county, begging to be allowed to spend the night in a cell.

By the time Jan's son received the treatment he needed, he and his parents and two sisters had been subjected to their second nightmare in five years, this one lasting twenty months from the time Jan had first sought help. He has now chosen to return to the family home and is well enough to ask his mother why on earth the hospital hadn't helped him when he went there; couldn't this have saved everyone a lot of time and expense? Meanwhile, he is not as well as could have been hoped; after so long without treatment, the medication that suited him the first time round has failed to help him this time. Others have produced worrying side effects.

Meanwhile, his elder sister commented bitterly during the worst part of this crisis that 'it feels is as if those who should be helping us have become the enemy!'.

Isn't it sad that some of our society's most traumatized families should feel so misunderstood and unsupported at times of crisis?

## A Minefield

Mary and Bill, whose daughter suffered a relapse thirteen years after her first breakdown found that this time each professional in turn ignored her medical history and sought to find reasons in her family relationships for her sudden abnormal behaviour.

Having kept well and lived a perfectly normal lifestyle for the past ten years or so, the young woman had decided she could now safely come off her medication. Within a very short time, her behaviour was such that in the course of the ten weeks leading up to her reinstatement on medication, a string of professionals became involved. These included no less than four psychiatrists, three GPs, three psychiatric registrars, six social workers and three community nurses; more professionals, in fact, than the family would hope to need in its lifetime. Dozens of hours of professional time were absorbed while her husband and her parents felt as if they were walking a minefield which had been prepared for them by the very people who should be helping them.

This capable young woman became more and more inadequate to protect herself and was constantly on the run, and generally neglecting herself, to the concern of various agencies in several different areas. Meanwhile, mental health professionals wanted to know why the family could only talk about *illness* and getting their daughter back on to medication? By the time this was eventually achieved, she was very deluded and depressed. Within days of the commencement of treatment she started to come out of her psychotic nightmare, as she had thirteen years earlier and within weeks she was well again.

She is one of many 'acute' sufferers with potential to remain completely well so long as she takes the drug which is the antidote to her chemical imbalance. She needs this in the same way that some diabetic sufferers need insulin. Most of all, she needs mental health professionals to understand that 'acute' sufferers do not have a label on them which says they are schizophrenic and they may be seen to be attractive, articulate and capable even when they are in fact rapidly losing touch with reality.

## 'Cliff Edge' Strategy

Perhaps it is not surprising that many relatives of sufferers come to believe that they live in a different world from the one inhabited by the professionals employed to help them. Often families are accused of fussing too much when they see the first signs of a threatened relapse in their loved one. Yet they are the ones who have everything to lose if no-one stops the rot.

First, they will have to witness the downward spiral of deterioration and misery entailed in waiting for the inevitable crisis. Second, they have to live with the nightmare fear that crisis can bring with it irreversible tragedy for their relative. The torment and terror of an untreated psychosis can lead to its victims harming themselves or attacking others whom they believe to be a threat to their safety. The latter can lead to disaster for themselves as well as for others, with long-term detention in a special hospital or prison perhaps hundreds of miles away from home.

Harming themselves can include risk of death. Estimated suicide figures in schizophrenia vary between ten and thirteen per cent, but such figures do not tell the whole story. Many of the self-inflicted deaths among students and other young people in the optimum risk age group may be due to an undiagnosed schizophrenic illness. Also some Coroners have shown a marked reluctance to record more than a verdict of 'misadventure' on many self-inflicted deaths in schizophrenia. Statistics aside, there are a distressing number of such deaths and most of us who are involved with this illness know from our day-to-day work experience just how common they are.

The death of one's child is said to be the ultimate tragedy. Julie tells how it feels when a son's death is due to the havoc wrought by this illness:

> SIMON
> He was lean, and mean
> and handsome
> But his mood swings ruled his life
> He lived alone, and walked alone –
> Had no need for a wife

He loved the natural things in life
The birds, the sun, the sky
He loved his mum and sister too
But his moods, they made him cry

He'd wreck his home, his life and ours
We'd start again from scratch
All was well, we'd hope, we'd pray
— Then came another patch

That mental illness ruled his head
His heart, his soul, his thought
It turned him to a violent beast —
His family were distraught

For years he fought this awful scourge
His family fought it too
We needed help, somewhere to turn
But friends were very few

They did not understand his moods
The language and the violence
We'd cry for help
We'd beg for help —
But were only met with silence

'He's just a lout, a lad on drugs'
Was all that they could utter
'The only place for folk like him
Is somewhere near the gutter'

Some doctors say
'there's nothing wrong'
They refuse him medication
His family try to comfort him
With love and dedication

He screamed at us, he threatened us,
He said he's take his life
He'd taken more just his share
Of anguish and of strife

They detained him in a mental home
He could not settle down
He wanted to come home again
To see his flat in town

They took him home for half a day
To his beloved flat
Nineteen floors up in the sky
They thought he'd cope with that

He stepped out on the balcony
And took a long last breath
Then hurled himself
two hundred feet
To meet his friend called DEATH

He fought his battle brave and well
Although he never won
I loved him then, I love him still
My SCHIZOPHRENIC son[4]

## An Undervalued Resource

Some professionals and other service providers are now geared to working with carers and to listening to them. All too often, however, families report experiences similar to those we have described in this chapter. When they have sought help they have either been ignored, or been told they are fussing too much. Yet it is families who have to pick up the pieces and provide much of our so-called 'community care'. Relatives can be helpful allies to professionals and other workers struggling to find ways of supporting sufferers in the community. Not only do many of them have the intelligence and insight to help us in our work, but they also have a special knowledge and experience of the problems raised by this illness.

We will be looking again at various examples of the powerlessness of families to protect the interests of their loved ones and themselves. Meanwhile, perhaps we can understand why so many carers speak warily of having to live their lives 'one day at a time' since they first became involved with this illness; for them, tomorrow may once again turn into a minefield.

# II
# Identifying and Meeting Needs

## CHAPTER 4

# Priorities for the Whole Family

We have noted the sort of things that may happen to individuals when they are becoming ill with schizophrenia and the way they can quickly become alienated from those around them. We have also noted what it feels like for families watching this phenomenon without understanding what they are seeing or what is causing it. Gradually, the family becomes more and more sure that the individual is ill and their own nightmare begins when they try to obtain acknowledgement that this is the case. It might be helpful at this stage to imagine how this might feel. Consider the following scenario:

Mandy, who is sixteen, has been behaving strangely for a couple of months. She is clearly desperately unhappy, she is avoiding her peers, she is snarling at the whole family but refusing to leave the house, she declines to sit down to any meals and grabs enormous amounts of stodgy food from the fridge (and she's always been so sensible about diet and proud of her figure).

Imagine Mandy is your sister. Increasingly, she spends the day lying on her bed and plays one or two of her tapes over and over again most of the night. She comes out of hiding when your mother is alone in the house and follows her around for hours without talking to her. A bright girl, she has not been to school for several weeks although she is obviously doing some studying at home. Her teachers are concerned that she should not miss too much school while studying for her 'A' levels but have noticed nothing strange about Mandy. Your parents' visit to the GP has not helped either.

Two seemingly interminable months later nothing has changed, except that no-one in the house seems able to get a good night's sleep any more and your sister is now looking haggard and throwing unprovoked tantrums. The GP says that she would need to come and ask for his help as he cannot intervene otherwise; perhaps the family can persuade her to come down to the surgery? This proves to be a non-starter; she becomes hysterical at the implication that she should see a doctor.

What would you be looking for at this point? How would you feel able to move forward from this 'stalemate' situation? Is there no alternative but to wait for a crisis to happen? If so, what sort of crisis? Could it prove an embarrassment and affect your sister's social standing in the community? Could further delays ruin her very real chances of a promising career following the studies she's always planned at college? Can the family stand many more sleepless nights and this feeling of walking a tightrope while Mandy is turning into a stranger? How is all this affecting her young brother and sister; Mum and Dad don't seem able to find much time just lately for these two and anyway your mother is exhausted. She's been getting even less sleep than the rest of you. How much longer can this go on?

Just how long do families very often wait for a professional response to their problem? The Northwick Park Study found that even where sick individuals were exhibiting extremely bizarre and, in some cases, clearly dangerous behaviour, delays in obtaining help often lasted over a year.[1] This could mean that Mandy's family might wait a very long time for help, perhaps long after her long-held plans for the future are in ruins. Certainly, eight years after the above study was carried out, it is not unusual to find families making the rounds from one agency to another in an attempt to get help. Their testimonies leave no doubt as to the nature of the eventual diagnosis nor that the sick person is seriously ill.

### Identifying Needs

What are the immediate priorities for such families? They are in desperate need of the services of the medical profession; it is doctors who can legitimately diagnose and treat a sick person. For this to be achieved, the first priorities have to be that those seeking help are able to obtain *acknowledgement*, accompanied by *explanations and a tentative diagnosis* and *treatment* as appropriate. Let's take a look at each of these priorities in turn:

### Acknowledgement That Something Is Wrong

Again and again families complain that their worries have not been taken seriously when they sought help; instead these were brushed aside. And yet, in most cases they were reporting a dramatic change in personality and lifestyle in a young person accompanied by apparent despair and unexplained hostility. Shouldn't this be cause for grave concern? Shouldn't serious attempts be made to rule out the possibility of a potentially devastating illness? Schizophrenia will attack one in every one hundred of us in our lifetime but, and this is so important, no less than eighty per cent of its victims by the time they are twenty-five years of age? This means that we should be proactive and expecting to find schizophrenia in a significant portion of each generation of the teenage/young adult population rather than pretending it doesn't exist. This is the main priority for families. They wish that professionals would pause a moment before producing platitudes. They do not need platitudes; they seek a professional response from a fellow human being who knows what is probably happening and who is prepared to act accordingly. Should this be too much to ask?

## Explanations

Even if fears of a schizophrenic illness should eventually prove groundless, families need to know as much as possible about it at the time of seeking help until such time as it can be demonstrated that something else is wrong and demanding attention. Some GPs no longer make home visits and some of those who do will refuse to call unless invited to do so by a patient who is by then intent on avoiding all doctors! If this is the case, then the family's evidence together with the individual's denial of any problem must give cause for concern. Some explanation is called for, albeit a tentative one. It is not in the interests of the individual concerned for the supporting network to be in a state of constant disarray, which is what happens when families don't know which way to turn.

It does not seem to have occurred to many of those working with schizophrenia that ignorance and denial lead to disempowerment. If we do not share our knowledge with those who have to cope with such an illness then we destroy their normal coping mechanisms and we deprive them of the privilege of controlling their own lives. This surely can't be what we are aiming for; to render so many families (perhaps one in every thirty in our society) impotent to help themselves, making them totally dependent on whatever services we can provide?

## Diagnosis and Treatment

Not unreasonably, families would like an early diagnosis and appropriate treatment for their loved one. It is important to rescue the unsuspecting victim sooner rather than later. Quite apart from humane considerations, can there be any excuse for delay? Increasingly desperate reactions to a psychotic nightmare can bring loss of dignity and reputation, perhaps destroying the individual's social standing and valued relationships as well as any longheld dreams and career plans. Deep despair and/or bullying 'voices' can, and do, lead to serious physical damage and sometimes death.

As pointed out earlier, untreated symptoms can heighten the risk of chronic illness involving irreversible damage. Furthermore, several pieces of research have revealed evidence that susceptibility to later relapses correlates with prolonged delays in receiving drug treatment[2]. It makes sense to assume that early intervention equates with damage limitation, particularly when we know that this is taken for granted with all illnesses except psychosis in general and schizophrenia in particular. This is puzzling because we know that the incidence of schizophrenia worldwide remains remarkably constant; by trying to ignore it we do not rid ourselves of the problem. We have learned to cope with cancer by intervening at the first signs of any worrying symptom so that this serious diagnosis can be ruled out or confirmed as quickly as possible. We do not say, 'let's wait and see because acknowledging this serious illness is too awful to contemplate'. We act so that we can limit the damage. Why can't we do the same for schizophrenia, which wreaks most of its damage on young people in the prime of life and which is treatable?

### Some More Priorities

Given that diagnosis and treatment will eventually be forthcoming, usually at the time of breakdown, what do families and other carers see as the main priorities at this point? A small survey[3] carried out recently with the help of members of a local NSF carers' group looked at services received around the time of the sufferer's first schizophrenic episode. The survey asked participants which of nine different services they received at this point and which of these they considered, in retrospect, to be a priority at that time. The nine services were as follows:

(1) Support for the family

(2) Full information about the illness

(3) Explanations about the sort of symptoms the sufferer had experienced and might again

(4) The role of medication in this illness

(5) The potential risk of further breakdown

(6) Advice as to what to do if the sufferer's health gave cause for concern in the future

(7) Advice about the benefits system and other practical services

(8) Introduction to self-help organizations and literature concerned with this illness

(9) Adequate information for *the sufferer* about the illness and how best to live with it.

Twenty-one families, out of a possible twenty-two, took part in this survey and over ninety per cent of respondents considered all of these services to be a priority *at the time of the first schizophrenic episode.* Just one family received most of these services and over eighty per cent received none of them at that time. Furthermore, fifty per cent have never received most of them, despite further opportunities for this when their relative has relapsed. These services were regarded as a priority from the start because they represented a preventive approach which respondents felt could have better enabled them to help and protect their relative. This small piece of research involved families who have a positive approach to their misfortune and who regularly contribute to the activities of a self-help group. Members of around half of these families are involved in voluntary work with long-term mental illness and most of them are survivors who have learned to cope with schizophrenia in the home for periods ranging from a couple of years to several decades. In short, they represent the sort of carers from whom the statutory services have the most to gain. The findings of this survey are valuable, perhaps making an excellent starting point from which to build up a partnership of caring. Let's take a look at what might be achieved if these nine services were 'delivered' at the appropriate time.

The family's morale would be boosted by initial supportive counselling; a couple of sessions should suffice. It is important that these include space for *listening.* The family need to talk through what they have been through and those working with the patient need to know about their experiences. After counselling, the family would be furnished with explanations about the illness in general and about the experiences of their relative in particular. They would be told about the role of the prescribed medication and that although this type of illness cannot be cured, it can be successfully treated in many cases. They would learn about those factors which are known to heighten risk of further breakdown and those which can expedite and help to maintain a lasting recovery. They would know that this sort of basic information would be shared with the sufferer, to create a proper under-standing of what has happened and of how to keep well in the future.

The family would be guided through the relevant basics of the benefits system and also given a brief account of resources in the local community, such as day care and sheltered housing facilities in case there should be a need for ongoing services of this nature then or later. Meanwhile, they would be given the names and addresses of organizations involved with this type of illness and offered an introduction to a local carer's group affiliated to one of these national bodies so that they could meet with other families with a similar experience if they chose to do so. Finally, they would be given details of any after-care planned for the sufferer, together with instructions as to the procedure to be followed if they should have any cause for concern in the future.

Wouldn't it be satisfying to work like this? It can be so rewarding to share one's knowledge and skills with those who will, after all, provide the main support system for our clients. As we noted, this sort of package is one that families would choose for themselves. For the purpose of this discussion, let us now assume that we have shared this important knowledge and information with those having to live with schizophrenia. What are the other priorities for these families?

### An End to Denial

Most families have struggled for months, sometimes years, to obtain an acknowledgement and explanation for their relative's problems. To their dismay and amazement, many then find that if and when there is a recurrence of the problem, they again meet denial when they express concern. This comes in several forms such as, for example:

(1) 'Don't you think you are fussing too much? We haven't noticed anything amiss, she's fine at the day centre.'

(2) 'She's obviously being attention-seeking and manipulative with you; with us, she's doing very well, but we have to be firm.'

(3) 'Yes, he may have had a schizophrenic illness, but there is no sign of psychosis now.'

These sort of responses, apart from being unhelpful, imply denial of an ever present risk of relapse in a schizophrenic illness. They also imply that those who know the individual best do not have a valuable contribution to make in combating this risk, despite work carried out by psychologists Max Birchwood, Jo Smith and their colleagues at All Saints Hospital in Birmingham which demonstrates that those closest to the sufferer can recognize the signs of relapse before others do so.[4]

## Listening And Hearing

An end to denial might result in families beginning to feel that those working with schizophrenia will listen to them and hear them. At present, this is not often the case. We have seen that they feel as if they are shouting into the wind when they try to obtain acknowledgement and help for a developing illness. This experience should not continue after a diagnosis has been achieved, but in many cases it does. We saw three examples of this in earlier chapters; let's take a further look at these:

### Jan's Son

Jan's first plea for help from her son's psychiatrist met with, 'Well, what do you expect with schizophrenia?'. This negative attitude reflects a belief that schizophrenia is big trouble, period. This is not necessarily the case and this approach is no more acceptable than one of denial as both tend to lead to masterly inactivity at just the times when this can be disastrous.

### John

His first episode of schizophrenia started with his constant complaints that he had physical problems. After all these had been investigated and come to nothing, he was eventually recognized as suffering with an acute form of schizophrenia and was treated for this. He made a good recovery and obtained the sort of work he had always hoped to do and he set up home a couple of years later. At this point, he also gave up taking his medication and within a few months he was reporting to his GP with all the same physical problems he had complained of the first time round. To his mother's horror, these were all investigated again despite the fact that she pointed out to the doctor what was happening; not only was her son complaining of the same physical problems, he was becoming hostile towards her again and stumbling from one crisis to another. She knows the GP to be a particularly caring man but he did not listen to what she was saying and her attempts to involve psychiatric professionals who had worked with her son previously were unsuccessful too. Later – much later – everyone concerned tried to stop the rot, but by then her son had lost his job (in this case a promising start to a longed for career) and his home. He is now living on the streets, alienated and mentally ill.

## Mary and Bill's Daughter

Her parents and husband pleaded for help from mental health professionals because she was obviously having a recurrence of her breakdown of thirteen years earlier. Not only could they see all the signs of this, but others could observe that this usually stable young woman was constantly on the run for weeks, neglecting herself and moving on as soon as anyone showed any concern for her mental health. In contrast, she kept seeking help for her physical health, regularly turning up at GPs' surgeries and hospital casualty departments. Again and again, her family pointed this out to mental health professionals but they did not listen. However, they *did* listen to everything the sufferer told them and this resulted in their believing extraordinary accusations made about the three most important people in her life. That they did so is an awesome testimony to the prevailing level of denial about this illness. Bill is concerned and perplexed by the denial he met while trying to get help for his daughter:

> 'With most of the professionals, it was as if they had an investment in proving she did not have this illness. I begun to believe in the end that they were quite mad.'

### Prompt Reaction

A prompt reaction is needed if help is to be given in time to prevent a long deterioration and a potentially damaging breakdown. As this is as important for families as being listened to and heard, they need to know that they can approach an individual or a department in a position to facilitate an immediate response. At present, 'the system' does not really allow for such provision but it certainly helps if the family is able to contact a professional who knows them and the sufferer well. This is one of the blessings of continuity.

### Continuity

For those families whose relative needs ongoing help, it is important that they should have as much continuity as possible from those working with the sufferer. Such continuity allows for the building up of relationships and, it is to be hoped, mutual trust and respect between the formal and informal carers. It is very tiring and dispiriting for the latter to have to 'start from scratch' again and again. It is also wasteful in time and effort when, as sometimes happens, a succession of workers flit in and out of a family's life, all with quite different approaches to their problems. When this happens with a 'difficult case', there is sometimes a marked tendency for the family to be left picking up the pieces each time.

## Proper Communication

As many families discover to their cost, some psychiatrists and GPs are adamant that medical confidentiality is sacrosanct. They may refuse to speak with carers unless the sufferer is present and agreeable to this. Bearing in mind the paranoid content of the illness, this can mean that it is those who have to care for really seriously ill sufferers who are often the very ones who are deprived of access to the doctors supervising their treatment. At a recent study day[5], one mother stood up and pointed out that this medical confidentiality seemed to be selective. When she and her husband wish to talk to their schizophrenic daughter's psychiatrist, he refuses and they never receive any help as to how best to look after her. However, when she became physically ill the previous year and needed surgery, that specialist called them into the hospital before her discharge to explain about the operation and how she would be affected by it and to tell them how they could best nurse her back to good health. They much appreciated this help and could only marvel at the absence of any need to protect the patient's confidentiality at the expense of her short-term needs when this confidentiality was said to be paramount where her long-term and more pressing needs were concerned.

Similarly, another carer pointed out immediately following this that sufferers were frequently discharged home with little or no notice and nothing in the way of information. She had recently asked some nursing friends if they would be prepared to take over a shift on a ward where the nurses on the previous shift had left without a proper hand-over session. They were horrified at this suggestion, so she explained that this is what happens to her, with the previous shift having lasted several weeks and hers lasting, if all goes well, for twelve months or longer. Not surprisingly, perhaps, she sees a lot of room for improvement in the present levels of communication. She believes that both parties – formal and informal carers – would benefit from knowing more about each other's experience of her daughter and, more important, the latter would gain from this.

## Mental Health Legislation

The Mental Health Act 1983 is meant to be used as a safety net for a small minority of the mentally ill who need to be admitted to hospital compulsorily. During the 1960s and 1970s this amounted to ten per cent of all in-patients, at a time when many sufferers were free to go into hospital when they felt the need or when their families or concerned professionals could persuade them that this was desirable. With the rapid closing of hospital beds, this facility is fast disappearing and it is not uncommon to hear of sufferers being told that coming into hospital is not appropriate when they have the insight to realise their need for it. This happened to Ben Silcock on more than one occasion before he eventually hit the media headlines by climbing into a lion's den in January 1993. Sadly, more and more of those sufferers who are admitted on a voluntary basis are often those who are coerced into this by professionals at a time of crisis, in preference to their being put on a section and formally detained. Thus families often wait months and months for the tragic deterioration of their relatives to be acknowledged, only to see them eventually persuaded to go into hospital on a voluntary basis after a mental health assessment. Time and again this achieves nothing, because patients then refuse to take the prescribed medication and 'vote with their feet', as we saw with Malcolm in Chapter 2 and with Jan's son in Chapter 3.

## Abuse of the Law?

The case of Jill's son is particularly worrying. This very young man was diagnosed as having a mild form of an acute schizophrenic illness five years ago. He was not admitted to hospital at that time as the prescribed oral medication was enough to control his symptoms and he made a good recovery. A year or so later, he decided he didn't need his medication any longer and started to deteriorate. His parents immediately sought help and the same psychiatrist who had treated him before put him back on the original medication with the same positive result. Eighteen months later, history repeated itself but this time he came under a new psychiatrist who was not convinced the boy was schizophrenic. In the delay which ensued, Jill and her husband watched their son become increasingly hostile and aggressive towards themselves and his sisters. Several months later, distraught and scared, he was clearly paranoid and became very destructive and threatening. His parents were becoming desperate and his sisters were, frankly, terrified. Twice during this period professionals came to the house to do a mental health assessment of him and twice this very sick boy became normal and lucid during their visits. Both times, the professionals left, advising Jill and her husband that their son was 'not sectionable' (because he was not exhibiting during the interview the behaviour that both family and other professionals had reported). They suggested that the parents should call the police if he did any more damage around the home or attacked them. Tragically, three painfully long weeks later, the young man went berserk and attacked one of his sisters. His father called in the police, as instructed, and, before he and his wife could take in what was happening, their son was in prison on remand. After several weeks – a period which this family will never forget nor forgive – he eventually found himself in the secure unit of a psychiatric hospital and back home again several months later after being treated with the drugs that he needs to keep him well. This quiet and gentle boy could have ended up being treated as a criminal.

This was indeed the fate of Tom's son; he stopped taking his medication, with the agreement of the professionals working with him, after keeping well on this for eighteen months or so. When his father found out, he protested as all those working with the young man knew that he had been in trouble with the police on two previous occasions before his illness had been properly acknowledged and treated. However, no attempt was made to get him back onto his medication, even when he asked to return to hospital seven months later. He was allowed to do this, but he discharged himself after three days, with 'They say I'm not ill; they're not going to do anything for me'. Three weeks later, he broke the law again. When he appeared in Court, the psychiatrist's report stated that this was a behavioural problem, not an illness. He went to prison, to the horror of his family, who then found that no arrangements had been made for his continuing psychiatric care on his return. All too often, the 'bad not mad' syndrome arises even when the 'badness' results from an approved withdrawal of medication.

## Care in the Community

Understandably, it has become an increasing priority of those trying to care for loved ones in the community that the law should be used to protect sufferers' interests and to make treatment available when they are too ill to accept this otherwise. This is the object of having mental health legislation and should never be by-passed in favour of resorting to criminal law nor in favour of inactivity. We saw examples of both in the case of Jill's son. Community Psychiatric Nurses (CPNs) were in and out of her house for weeks because the young man was becoming so ill and yet professionals working with the law pronounced him 'not sectionable' even while they were advising the parents to call in the police next time he became violent. This sort of practice is quite unacceptable when the Mental Health Act 1983 allows for an individual to be sectioned *in the interests of his health*.[6] It does not say anywhere that the patient must first demonstrate in front of those doing the mental health assessment that he is a danger to himself or others. Few psychotic sufferers would ever do that.

Perhaps it is not surprising that it has become a priority for families involved with this illness that professionals working with the Mental Health Act 1983 should know their law and use it to protect sufferers from unnecessary damage.

## Summing up

In this chapter we have looked at the main needs of families and these may be briefly summed up as:

- Acknowledgement
- Diagnosis and treatment
- Supportive counselling
- Information and explanations for all concerned
- Continuing acknowledgement instead of denial
- An immediate response to appeals for help
- Continuity and effective communication
- Proper use of the law.

Let us now take a look at further priorities, this time highlighted by sufferers themselves.

## CHAPTER 5

# Priorities for Sufferers

The needs of the family as a whole have been considered before those identified by sufferers, as the latter are initially unable 'to fight their corner' until they are rescued from their psychosis. At this stage they are dependent on others achieving this for them and ensuring that they receive treatment for their schizophrenic illness. What, then, are their initial needs when this is achieved?

## A Lifeline

As we have seen, sufferers frequently use a family member – often the mother – as a lifeline during the period leading up to their breakdown. Once diagnosed and in hospital they have a desperate need to have a similar one-to-one relationship with a member of staff whom they can trust and turn to for reassurance. However, they regularly complain that it is as if everyone simply sits back and waits for the medication to work rather than making use of that time to build up a relationship with the patient. This is a tragic waste of resources as sufferers desperately need someone to whom they can relate and whom they can trust when they are recovering from a breakdown; someone who can provide reassurance and opportunities to test reality.

Sally is an attractive and talented woman who has a remarkable gift for bringing comfort and cheer to those around her. She has suffered with schizophrenia for thirty years and the illness has played havoc with her life for most of that time. Happily, her recovery during the past three years has been such that she has been able to help professionals and laypeople alike to understand about the misery of an untreated illness and about the factors that have gradually led to her own survival. Sally wishes that:

'hospital staff and others involved with sufferers recovering from a breakdown could be aware of their sense of *remoteness* from the rest of the world and the feelings of total isolation that go with it'.

She says this is aggravated by the 'almost overwhelming "inner world" of schizophrenia which serves to maintain a frightening detachment from reality'. She believes that the building up of trust in a 'one-to-one' relationship at the time of breakdown is essential to a proper recovery and that, ideally, this should be a continuing relationship on which the sufferer can rely until such time as recovery is well under way.

### Reassurance and Reality Testing

During the period in which sufferers are trying to get hold of reality they need constant reassurance that everything 'is now all right' and that their lingering fears are unfounded. If encouraged to do so, they will frequently ask for reassurance. If this comes from a trusted source, it will provide them with some peace, a commodity they are badly lacking and very much needing. This respite from torment might last just ten minutes or so initially, but it will last for very much longer as their confidence returns. Meanwhile, they can also seek clarification about the boundaries between their fantasy world and what is happening around them, thus enabling them to test reality and their own perspectives on this.

We looked at some of the experiences of Tina and Pat in the second chapter of this book. Both are intelligent young women who have confirmed the reports of many others with this illness that 'this need to talk with someone on the ward and to have reassurance is seen as *attention-seeking behaviour*, staff tell you to go away and stop bothering them'.[*] When this happens, sufferers are deprived of the means of meeting a first priority in becoming well again. Significantly, they are also seriously undermined at a time when this illness has already ravaged their self-esteem. The restoration of one's self respect in such circumstances is dependent upon first receiving acceptance and respect from others.

### Diagnosis and the Dignity of a sick Role

If we avoid the use of a diagnosis, which is quite common on hospital wards these days, then there is a danger that we treat patients as if they are 'difficult'

---

[*]　It is worrying that the labelling of patients as 'attention-seeking' in such circumstances may reflect a need in some professionals to distance themselves from their work. What can be more important than paying attention to their patients?

rather than seriously ill. Not surprisingly, sufferers very much resent the use of derogatory labels to describe behaviour provoked by their illness; labels such as 'manipulative', 'attention-seeking', and 'demanding'. Such labels imply a choice for the individual; they imply that he or she is *choosing* to be 'difficult'. A diagnosis implies no such choice; instead it provides a reason for the patient's behaviour and therefore an explanation for what is happening. Whereas the above labels imply childish or inappropriate behaviour, a diagnosis of schizophrenia defines symptoms which in turn explain predictable responses in the patient. In short, it is more dignified to receive recognition of one's illness when one is ill.

Similarly, it is common for a non-diagnosis such as 'personality disorder' to be used in place of a treatable diagnosis. This is a *label* which is allocated to over a third of all schizophrenia sufferers at some time and which is deeply resented and understandably so. It is a label rarely arrived at after careful consideration of the individual's pre-morbid personality. It is also a label which is often eventually discarded when successful treatment proves it to be a nonsense.

## Explanations and Information

Understandably, sufferers have an urgent need for explanations about what has been happening to them. These should include the general features of a schizophrenic illness and clarification about vitally important matters in each individual's own experience – such as Pat's belief that she had regularly heard her father's voice planning to kill her. How could she get on with the rest of her life without understanding this experience? Such explanations and resultant discussions can be useful for all concerned. This includes those working with sufferers as they can then appreciate the full content and extent of the individual's delusional ideas at the time of breakdown. As sufferers start to get a grasp of reality, they are hungry for information about the illness and about its meaning for their future, given that this is shared at the right pace and in a deservedly positive manner. It is at this point that they can begin to develop insight into their illness and this is the stuff of survival.

## Insight

The gaining of insight into one's illness is the turning point in a proper recovery. Without this insight, sufferers continuously walk a tightrope, even if they seem to be making progress and resuming a normal lifestyle. Without this insight, they remain victims of the delusional ideas of their illness and blame those around them for what has happened to them and for 'incarcerating' them in hospital. Without this insight, they do not believe they have ever been ill and any reference to illness in the future may be like a red flag to a bull. They do not understand that the medication has been responsible for their 'recovery', but believe that those around them suddenly stopped persecuting and obstructing them. This is not a sound basis from which to get on with the rest of your life, nor is it a happy one.

Stephen, whose paper on medication is featured later in this chapter, has said recently that he believes the gaining of insight for sufferers should be the most important goal for those treating their illness.

## Comment

We have now highlighted the initial priorities for sufferers once their illness is acknowledged and these include the need for:

- A lifeline
- Reassurance and opportunities to test reality
- Respect
- The dignity of a diagnosis
- Explanations and information
- Gaining insight into what has happened.

What do survivors see as the main priorities for getting on with 'life after schizophrenia'?

### The Changing of Attitudes

The extent to which sufferers come to terms with a diagnosis of schizophrenia is initially influenced by their perception of how society sees them. I never quite realized just how destructive this perception could be until I read Graham's poem, written eighteen months after his breakdown:

> THINGS AIN'T WHAT THEY USED TO BE!
> There's no future for a schizophrenic;
> Doesn't it just make you sick?
> We're not thick but we take some unjust verbal STICK.
> There's no future for a schizophrenic;
> Other people just take the mick
> Some of us have got degrees;
> One of them is a friend called Nick.
> Other people belittle us
> Which gets on our wick.

Why do they do this,
When they don't even know us,
And don't know what makes us tick?
Doesn't it just make you sick?

Your former friends run away from you.
Your true friends are few.
When you're a schizophrenic,
You don't gain anyone new,
And those who occasionally do
Are schizophrenic too.
And this just makes you worse,
You feel paranoid and start to fret and stew.

Once you've heard voices,
You're left with no choices;
Perhaps you'll never find a girl friend
Or an understanding wife.
When they know you've had a mental illness
They'll never give you a job,
So all you can do is sob.
You know you're as good as them,
Hence you feel like you've been robbed.

You're faced with a life on Income Support
Facing up to this reality is the biggest battle you've fought
Because you know your prospects are nought.
As money's always short.
You'll never be able to own your own home
So you feel as tall as a garden gnome.
The way things are you can barely afford to buy a comb,
And roam from group home to group home!

People treat you like an alien
This weighs around your neck like a ton
It's like having no heat or no sun
And all you want to do is run
The only consolation is there's little stress and worry
Life is leisurely; there's no hurry.
I only hope that one day God will say 'sorry'.

Fortunately, this young man finds life considerably more rewarding now than he expected he would two years ago. Graham's words arrested my attention because they demonstrated just how much of his suffering had been due to his perception of the stigma surrounding schizophrenia and, more important, to his *perception* of society's attitude to himself and others like him. At this point, we can see how vital it is that those working with sufferers *communicate* their acceptance and respect for them if they are to cope with society's attitude to mental illness.

## Communication

Right from the start of their recovery, this perception is fuelled for sufferers in all sorts of ways. For example, the implications of silence about the diagnosis among the professionals working with them are enormous. One well recovered sufferer has pointed out that the patient feels *less than human* and decides 'I must be a hopeless case because no one will discuss my problems or give me any chance to respond intelligently'[1]. This lack of proper communication gives all the wrong messages, as do, of course, the use of derogatory labels.

Another example of ineffective communication was pointed out to me some years ago by a young man just recovered from a first schizophrenic episode. He asked me:

> 'Why couldn't they have explained where I was when they admitted me? I was told it was a hospital, but knew it couldn't be so because everyone was fully dressed, most of them watching television, and there were no beds nor nurses in sight. This all fed into my delusionary system.'[2]

This new sufferer had no conception at all of something very familiar to all who work with mental illness; he had never seen the inside of a psychiatric hospital and no-one had explained that he had been admitted to anything other than a general hospital. It took a long time before he was prepared to relate to anyone at all in his new surroundings. However, it is quite possible that this may not have been noted, let alone understood, as sufferers are so often left to their own devices in hospital.

It is ironic that so many of those who work with this illness have been led to believe that sufferers do not wish to, or are unable to, communicate with those around them. This has not been my experience with any individuals who have the acute form of schizophrenia and these, of course, make up a significant proportion of short psychiatric hospital admissions nowadays. Not only do sufferers have the ability to communicate effectively with those around them, particularly in a 'one-to-one' situation, but they can teach everyone more about this illness than any text-book.

## An Appreciation of the Role of the Medication

Probably the most important lesson for those who have had a schizophrenic illness is coming to terms with the need for the drugs that can help them survive this. Many have to persevere indefinitely with these and most, if not all, learn this the hard way, by trial and (sometimes costly) error. Stephen has written a paper on his own experiences because he wants others to find an easier way through this particular minefield than he did. He has been suffering from schizophrenia for a decade or more and is now, in his own words, 'happy and stable'.

MY SCHIZOPHRENIC ILLNESS – An Important Part of my Treatment

'Initially I became ill when I was taking street drugs and was seen by a psychiatrist at my bedsit. Medication was soon prescribed for my schizophrenia, which I tried and didn't really like taking. I had become suspicious of my carers, parents and friends, which was a symptom of my paranoid state. Seeing many different 'understudy' doctors and nurses didn't help!

I continued to take street drugs now and then, especially cannabis and amphetamines which imitated the effects of the illness in my case. I know now that these street drugs continued to cut across the medication like a sledgehammer, so the treatment didn't work for me as well as it could have. I found that taking medication was fraught with problems whilst I continued to take them. Crucially, I didn't really give the medication a chance to allow it to work for me and take me to the point where I could gain insight into my illness and realise this was what was causing my problems. This insight eventually came about two years ago as I write and I really feel better for it. I have been lucky with side-effects which only dogged me initially and, although I am on a relatively high dose of medication, there are no side effects worrying me now.

A good few years after my initial illness, I stopped taking medication and relapsed badly into another breakdown. The doctor decided too late that I needed help and I had to be admitted to hospital under a section of the Mental Health Act, which I found very frightening; I wished I had never stopped taking the medication!

After five years, I am happy and well, but the 'climb back' was long and difficult. Eventually my doctor and I found a marvellous balance of medication for me and I have never looked back since this time. Although I still have some symptoms, the medication helps me cope with them fairly easily. I have declined to cut down the medication as someone suggested because I never want to feel again the way I did when I was taken into hospital.

Over recent years I have taken responsibility for my own health. I have avoided all habit-forming medications such as sleeping tablets. I have been careful to respect the medication prescribed for me and to take the right dose at the right time and I ask for help if my symptoms become troublesome. I do recommend others with this type of illness to persevere until they can find the right mix and dose of medication with the help of their doctor. It has been worth it for me!'

Tina is another sufferer who has struggled for years with an innate reluctance to take medication. She started, slowly, to win that battle the day the two of us stood in the grounds of a local hospital after she had yet again stopped taking her medication. She pointed out to me in terror a tree that was talking to her and threatening her. We have often laughed since about this moment, but it wasn't funny at the time and she never forgot my quiet, exasperated comment, 'Look, this could be the rest of your life if that's what you want'. Having gradually won her own personal struggle with coming to terms with her continuing need for medication, she has attempted to explain why she believes sufferers come off their medication:

WHY DO WE STOP?

'No-one really knows why we stop taking medication, but I'd like to put my opinion across to you, being a sufferer myself and knowing many others.

I think we know deep down that we are going to become ill when we do this, but you have to have a dream that it will work and one day you will become 'NORMAL'; if you lose that dream then you have nothing left. Friends, relatives and professionals (well, most!) constantly remind you of the fact that you need your medication and deep down inside you know yourself that this is true. However, no-one can understand how the medication can make you feel unless they have actually experienced it; the drowsy feelings, the days when all you do is sleep, bring feelings of depression because you feel useless to society. You feel a failure. So what do you do to change this? Simple, you try to be 'NORMAL' by reducing or coming off your medication... when this doesn't work, you start again!

For ten years or so I have been off and on, more frequently on, medication and I am now beginning to achieve some of the things I want out of life, but, by God, its been a hard struggle! I have a little saying which I would like to share with any sufferer who reads this:

> DETERMINATION, DEDICATION and a little MEDICATION: *determination* to keep on fighting, *dedication* from friends, relatives and professionals who stick by you and, of course, *medication*, because in the end that is what keeps us well.'

Such insight can take a long time to achieve!

## Respect for the Family Unit

When asked what she considers to be the main priority for individuals who have had a schizophrenic illness, Sally has no doubts about this and says simply 'the support of a family. It is so sad to see what happens to those who lose this'. She believes that ensuring that families have the 'means with which to cope' should be a first priority. She is one of several survivors I know who are determined to find a way to help carers to understand what schizophrenia feels like from within so that they can better appreciate how this affects relationships that really matter to sufferers.

Similarly, Pat has brought up an issue which many recovered sufferers and their families would heartily endorse. Why, she wants to know, do those carrying out a mental health assessment assume that carers and sufferers are suddenly at war with one another? Why do they take so literally the delusional accusations of sufferers about the very people they are happy to live with or be with much of the time when they are not psychotic? She does not understand how professionals can work alongside families and be glad that they are there to support sufferers until such time as there is a crisis and the families desperately need their support. She points out:

> 'It is at such times that it is in the interests of the whole family that the crisis be resolved and yet professionals tend to take sides as if this was a rational difference of opinion instead of the re-emergence of the sufferer's psychosis.'

Pat wants to see formal and informal carers working in partnership at such times for the mutual benefit of everyone concerned.

## Continuity

This important matter comes up again. We have already noted how much individuals with this type of illness value continuity and Sally feels that an ongoing 'one-to-one' relationship with a doctor, nurse, or other worker is a real priority for sufferers. It has certainly been so in her case. Unfortunately, the natural movement of staff seems to have escalated recently as a result of re-organization, sectorization and re-sectorization *ad infinitum*, making such continuity quite rare and even leading to some confusion as to who belongs to whom. It is not unknown for some patients to find that they have temporarily slipped through the net and have no supervising doctor while others are being offered appointments by no less than three. No-one is likely to feel reassured under these circumstances.

One of the main 'bones of contention' about lack of continuity among recovered sufferers is their experience of out-patient clinic supervision. Out-patient appointments, usually at three- or six-monthly intervals, can be their one remaining contact with the mental health services. As a general rule, the individual is sooner or later allocated to junior doctors rather than to the supervising psychiatric consultant. The official viewpoint is that this system frees the senior doctor for new cases or for particularly difficult ones, while providing a variety of experience for junior doctors in training. Many sufferers do not see it quite this way. Ralph is one of these.

As he explains, Ralph sees each doctor once or twice only, which gives no opportunity for the development of any sort of rapport or trust. The interview usually consists of his being asked several 'stock-in-trade' questions concerned with his appetite and his sleep pattern and whether or not he goes out socially, or perhaps has a job. He has little interest in answering such questions, but would like the chance to answer others such as 'How are you feeling? How have you been coping?' He finds that these are answered for him, with 'Oh, well, you're doing fine!' when this is sometimes patently not so. Although reasonably well much of the time, this is not always the case and on several occasions Ralph has tried in vain to explain how unwell he has been feeling. On one such occasion he managed to say to yet another new doctor that he had been feeling depressed for some weeks. He found her quick reply, 'Oh, what makes you think you might be depressed?' so off-putting that he did not enlarge on this. He assumed from her tone that the doctor was suggesting he knew little about such matters. Although he may well have been right, a possibly premature assumption would be less likely if he had some prior knowledge of the individual on the other side of the desk. She did not, anyway, press the point. In short, because Ralph did not know the doctor and she did not know him, effective communication became impossible.

Ralph perseveres with his appointments because this seems to be the responsible thing to do and because he hopes that one day someone will attempt to monitor his drug treatment, which has remain unchanged for many years. He tells me his file is a thick one, resulting from a couple of severe breakdowns a long time ago. Despite this and although he is well enough to have held down a good job for many years, he assumes that the doctors find him a boring case. If so, he is in good company; few of their patients seem to feel that the doctors take the trouble to acquaint themselves with even the basics of their history before meeting them. I have known a few who have stormed out of these sessions, extremely upset by an innocent, if insensitive, remark from a stranger. One client did so after being asked 'Have you ever wanted to kill anyone?' Perhaps it is a pity that she resisted an almost overwhelming temptation to reply, 'No, not until now!'

Not unreasonably, sufferers want their progress to be monitored by someone they know and who is conversant with their history. For some, these out-patient sessions represent the *only* opportunity they have to talk to someone about their illness, having to 'live a lie' the rest of the time. They find it difficult to conceive that these short and stereotyped interviews can be any more profitable for doctors in training than for themselves.

## Equal Opportunities for Work

Although we live at a time when many employers can boast an equal opportunities policy, it is noticeable that things have not improved for individuals with a psychiatric record and, in particular, for those who have suffered from a psychotic illness. Chris Heginbotham, a former director of MIND, has pointed out:

> 'Few people realize there is no redress for disabled people. No equivalent of the Sex Discrimination Act or the Race Relations Act exists and any disabled person can be discriminated against with impunity'[3]

Not only are employers wary of taking on someone with a disability they cannot really understand, *or see*, they are anxious to avoid taking on a pension risk. Medical advisers screen out any applicants who might pose such a risk, with questions covering a lifetime's medical history and including questions on whether or not medication is still prescribed (in the erroneous belief that this will not only indicate the illness involved, but also the seriousness of it). Thus, individuals with a history of mental illness are expected to declare this even if it occurred decades before, while the law protects criminals from this sort of probing into their law-breaking activities once five years has passed. Tina's experience of four years ago is a particularly bad example. She was offered general nursing training by a health authority on condition that *she came off her medication in time for the start of the course.* She was given to understand she was unemployable because she was still taking medication. Fortunately, sanity prevailed and she chose to stay well and so turned down this senseless and immoral offer. Only she knows how much pain this caused her...

All in all, discrimination in employment against individuals who have suffered a schizophrenic illness is disturbingly common. Most sufferers do not reach the interview stage of recruitment if they are truthful on their application forms. The alternative choice, of omitting to mention their medical history, can result in having to 'live a lie' in one's day-to-day life and in instant dismissal if this is detected. This is hardly an ideal situation for recovered sufferers trying to confirm that there is 'life after schizophrenia' and it is certainly not calculated to help them stay well.

Needless to say, this situation leads to deep frustration for many able individuals who have a great deal to offer. Sometimes sufferers do have the chance to demonstrate this when they manage to obtain good jobs 'via the back door'; they usually turn out to be valuable employees not least because they have so much more to gain than the rest of us by proving their worth.

### An End to all Discrimination

Discrimination against individuals who have had a schizophrenic illness covers a much wider span than the blocking of employment opportunities and there is little wonder that many spend their time trying to deny and abort a diagnosis which provokes so much intolerance.

### Quality of Life

What are the practical factors that contribute most to the everyday quality of life of sufferers? Those that come up again and again are:

(1) Satisfactory level of income

(2) Satisfactory accommodation

(3) Rewarding and stimulating occupation

(4) Supportive social network.

Clearly, the way these needs are met will depend to a great extent on the extent of the ability of sufferers to fend for themselves after a schizophrenic illness. While some sufferers will find they can sooner or later pick up the threads of their previous lives, many more will be dependent to a greater or lesser extent on services which can be provided for them. For the remaining ten per cent of all those who have schizophrenia, their overwhelming need will be for ongoing and full-time intensive care. With schizophrenia, the lifestyle of sufferers can range from potential normality through to severe disability and this brings us back to the greatest need of all for its victims; *damage limitation* in an eminently treatable illness.

## CHAPTER 6

# Meeting Needs Identified by Families

In Chapter 4, we looked at the needs of families and other carers trying to cope with schizophrenia and noted that these are never greater than when the illness first attacks its victim. As actress Stephanie Cole put it at the start of 1994:

> 'A loving family can be plunged into a living hell. My family struggled to cope for years...'.[1]

As we have seen, the first priority for the family at this time is to get health professionals to listen and acknowledge the seriousness of the problem. How can we start to meet this need without the long delays which currently take place?

## Acknowledgement

Acknowledgement of the problem is quite basic if we accept that we have no choice but to acknowledge it if we cannot satisfy ourselves *that there isn't one*. This can only happen if we first investigate carefully the reason for the concern of those presenting the problem. To do this, we have to listen and to hear everything they have to say, while clarifying the following points:

(1) What was the 'pre-morbid picture'; what sort of personality did the individual have before the problem begun?

(2) What sort of personality changes have taken place?

(3) What sort of changes in lifestyle have taken place?

(4) Were there any incidents leading up to these changes which might have contributed to them in any way, i.e., a bereavement or other loss, physical illness, or surgery?

(5) Is there evidence of abuse of drugs, solvents or alcohol? If so, has this coincided approximately with the changes described?

(6) Could this be an adolescent crisis to which the family might be over-reacting? If we think this is the case, we must be able to define the problem to the satisfaction of ourselves and the family.

If (1), (2) and (3) represent dramatic changes in personality and lifestyle which cannot be explained by (4), (5) or (6), then this narrows the field considerably. If, however, (4) is applicable then consideration should be given to offering appropriate assessment and counselling. If (5) is applicable, then the timing may be important; has a habit developed in an attempt to escape the sort of frightening experiences connected with a psychotic illness or could the habit itself explain what is happening now? If the latter applies, then, again, assessment and counselling is called for. If (6) seems applicable – that is, after considering the table of possible pointers below – then again assessment and counselling is called for. In other words, if we make this sort of structured analysis, it quickly becomes clear that a 'let's wait and see' approach is inappropriate in all cases.

Having eliminated factors which may be important in (4) and (5) and, possibly (6), we should also note if the individual declines to speak with us or refuses to acknowledge any problem other than that of 'the family fusses too much' variety. If this is the case, we should then turn again to the evidence in (1), (2) and (3) above; if there have been dramatic and unexplained changes,then we would expect a family to be 'fussing' and we should share their concern. We have now come back full circle.

## Possible Indicators of an Underlying Illness

What sort of signs might indicate the presence of the cluster of symptoms associated with a schizophrenic illness. The sort of pointers we should look for may be divided into three groups;[2] (1) physical, (2) behavioural and (3) anecdotal, as follows:

### Physical

- Sleep disturbance, especially turning night into day
- Lacks energy; quickly tires
- Changed eating habits
- Inability to make eye contact
- Change of menstruation pattern in young women
- Uncharacteristic complaints of all sorts of physical ailments

- Haggard features and haunted/stary eyes.

### Behavioural

- Withdrawal from friends and from favourite activities
- Suddenly spending hours in own room, perhaps with curtains drawn closed during daytime
- Clinging to one person (often mother) in previously independent person
- Refusal to eat with others
- Uncharacteristic avoidance of TV or radio
- Uncharacteristic lack of interest or pride in appearance and personal hygiene
- Unexplained bouts of hostility
- Use of bad language that is quite out of character.

### Anecdotal

- Reports of unexplained unhappiness in the individual
- Reports of a worrying and unexplained change in personality and lifestyle
- Reports from those closest to the individual that *something is different, something is wrong.*

If a cluster of such signs is evident (and, clearly, each on its own might have very little significance), then the right questions should elicit whether or not predictable symptoms, discussed in Chapter 2, might be the underlying cause for them.

We may have now found strong indications that the problem might be schizophrenia; a common and treatable illness which should demand our immediate attention. We now have a responsibility to acknowledge a problem that a family has brought to us and make it our business to obtain further assessment and diagnosis for the individual concerned. If we are members of the medical profession then we are already on the way to reaching a tentative diagnosis and, more important, to *providing treatment.* If we are not members of the medical profession, then we need to make a careful note of our findings and make these available to a medical colleague or the family's GP, as appropriate.

## Diagnosis

Although there are recognized diagnostic measures available to the medical profession such as the *Diagnostic and Statistical Manual of Mental Disorders*, (DSM III), there is also a longstanding and widespread tendency to miss or avoid diagnosing schizophrenia even when patients are eventually admitted to hospital. Research in Denmark[3] demonstrated that only fifty per cent of all new male sufferers and forty per cent of all new female sufferers in 1972 were diagnosed as having schizophrenia on their first admission to hospital. Two decades later, this phenomenon is still a common one and it is not at all unusual to meet sufferers whose diagnosis was not established until their second admission to hospital. There seem to be four reasons for these dangerous delays:

### (1) Over-emphasis on avoiding a stigmatizing 'label', as some individuals will have no further episodes of the illness

As we have seen, avoidance of the diagnosis can leave the victims of this illness unprotected and more likely to relapse. As for the argument that some will have no further breakdowns, they too need to know what has happened to them as the rest of their lives can be blighted by residual and unexplained symptoms.[4] It is, anyway, a cruel irony to delay diagnosis because of the dangers of labelling when this leaves the individual unprotected and more likely to eventually develop a disabling illness for all to see.

### (2) Claims that it is very difficult to establish the presence of this illness

This is understandable when assessment so often relies on the testimony and performance of the sick person. It is well known that individuals experiencing a psychotic nightmare are notoriously skilled at avoiding detection in the short term when they know they are being assessed. Most can keep up this pretence that 'all is well thank you' for up to an hour or so because they believe they are fighting for their lives; that they are in terrible danger. They behave exactly as any of us would in the same circumstances and are poised ready for 'flight', lucid and charming and able to cope with all comers, provided that they are asked innocuous questions which cause them no problems or allowed to by-pass difficult ones. This illness will seem difficult to diagnose until such time as the testimony of those closest to the individual is sought and a structured approach, similar perhaps to the kind outlined above, is followed every time. It is usually the case that adequate evidence is available for the asking and that referral to this will expedite the provision of urgently needed treatment.

*(3) Over-emphasis on adhering carefully to currently recognized criteria such as the DSM III's requirement that a six month 'qualification priod' has to take place before a diagnosis of schizophrenia should be made[5]*

Emphasis on time factors and other such practicalities in *DSM III* represents a responsible effort to attempt to standardize definitions of this illness. Standardization can be important for research purposes but is much less so for an individual who desperately needs care and treatment. These needs should be paramount; if necessary the diagnosis can be provisional and confirmed later, as appropriate. Meanwhile, the family and individual concerned should be kept informed and need to have explanations of the possible implications of such an episode.

*(4) Similarities between schizophrenia and other conditions, such as manic depressive illness and a schizo-affective disorder*

Work carried out by the Northwick Park Hospital team suggests that these may all be part of a continuum of conditions, with certain symptoms in common which are responsive to the same neuroleptic drugs.[6] It may be a sad irony that delays in diagnosis can result in the withholding of such medication.

## Assessment

It is only if those who do the assessing are aware of all the changes that have taken place and the sort of events that have led up to the assessment interview being sought that they can know which questions to ask. Too often they have to rely on questions such as 'Have you been hearing voices?'. For first-time sufferers this is a waste of time. Even if they have been hearing voices, they are probably unaware of this phenomenon. Usually, such a question merely confirms the individual's suspicions that the rest of the world has gone mad. For existing sufferers, it is also a waste of time; if they are trying to avoid being seen to be relapsing, they will not be admitting to this 'give away' symptom.

However, if the doctor or other assessor is acquainted with feedback from those closest to the individual or, failing that, from colleagues, then all sorts of questions can be potentially profitable, for example:

'Your mother tells me you are a talented musician but have given up studying and playing the piano over the past few months; I am wondering why that is?'

'I gather you spend all your leisure time at home alone now; have you always done that?' or 'I understand you've given up going out with your old friends now; how do you think they feel about that?'

'Your GP tells me you have been to see him rather a lot over recent months. It sounds as if you've not been feeling at all well; what do you think might be the matter?' or 'I am wondering if you know why your GP thinks you might need my help?'

'Your family seem concerned that you don't join them at mealtimes any more or eat proper meals; I'm wondering what has brought about this change in your eating habits?' or 'I gather from your family that you are up and about most of the night and go to bed just before the rest of us get up. Why do you think that is?'

'Your family tell me that if they switch on the television this upsets you, but you used to watch it avidly. What is it that is bothering you with this?' or 'Your mother tells me you will not let her draw the curtains even in broad daylight; I am wondering why this is?'

Quite apart from the main motive in asking these 'sensitive' questions, all of which put demands on someone seeking to deny there is a problem, they also have potential in enabling the individual to talk about familiar things that are affecting everyday life as it is being experienced in a developing psychosis. If some sort of understanding of 'where the individual is' can be achieved, then it is the later, interpretative, questions that may be the most rewarding:

'I mentioned the curtains just now because I was wondering if you sometimes feel you are being watched through the window; I've met several people who have had that fear.'

Finally, if the assessor keys into the unhappiness and fear which is never far below the surface, this can sometimes lead to acknowledgement from the individual that things are not as they should be. It helps to remember that sufferers often express relief immediately after others take over responsibility for their lives. Bella, a nurse for many years and a CPN during the twelve years up to her retirement in 1990, has commented on how obvious this has become when she has several times arrived on the scene at the end of a mental health assessment:

'Sufferers are notoriously skilled at pretending all is well when this is not the case. Sometimes clients have told me later "and then you walked in the door!" after they had just convinced the doctor or another professional that the family was making a fuss about nothing. The anxious protests of the relatives had been ignored – an all too common occurrence – and the situation was rapidly worsening when my client was actually relieved to see someone arrive who would see through the pretence and do something.'

## Professional Responsibility

It is a matter of some concern that unless the professional doing the assessment is determined to get to the bottom of the misery that is being reported, then the suffering can go on and on. I was once asked to do a mental health assessment on a woman in her thirties whose husband was becoming quite desperate about her bizarre and increasingly dangerous behaviour. Two colleague ASWs had each pronounced her as 'unsectionable' and gone on their way, leaving a battlefield behind them, without offering any solution or further support.

I was not surprised to find this attractive woman lucid and anxious to make me feel welcome. She made me a cup of tea and we talked for forty minutes or so. Apart from a sharp, dismissive, 'I'm too tired to remember' in response to my query about a violent episode on the previous day, following the departure of the second ASW, she readily agreed that she had not been coping for some time with all sorts of day-to-day tasks. She explained carefully and repeatedly that this was because she was 'so tired all the time'. Unless I focused my mind determinedly on the chaos reported by her despairing husband and the evidence of this all around us, it would have been very easy to accept her explanations and to have too walked away from this couple's distress. It was not until I eventually asked her why she thought she was so tired, *because clearly we must do something about this*, that her very convincing veneer cracked. She sprung at my throat, vividly reminding me that it is always more exacting and dangerous to persevere when making an assessment than to let sufferers in need of treatment and care persuade you that they are fine, thank you! Several months later I was reminded, too, that they have to depend on us to protect them from their illness when this woman came to seek me out to thank me for making it possible for her to resume her old life and to save her marriage. This is not the first time that I have had ample proof that we cannot justify avoiding use of the mental health legislation on the grounds that we might spoil our relationship with the sufferer; a not uncommon excuse for masterly inactivity!

Assuming acknowledgement, diagnosis (albeit tentative), and appropriate treatment have been achieved, we now come to the package of nine services that carers have highlighted as being crucial at this stage[7]. Let's take a closer look at each of these:

## (1) Support for the Family

Many families members have never had any contact with the agencies working with the sufferer, let alone received any supportive counselling. In some cases, the lives of these unacknowledged victims have been savaged by this illness and they have eventually voted with their feet and broken away from the family. One father, desperately fighting the temptation to run, has written to me, pointing out:

> 'there has to be a regime which allows all those who are long term participants in the drama to continue with an acceptable level of compromise to their personal needs. If the demands on any one (family member) are too great then breakdown of the group will occur'.[8]

Family breakdown more often than not leads to one of two scenarios; (a) an unsupported and socially isolated sufferer or (b) a deserted and isolated mother trying to care for a sick son or daughter into her old age. Both scenarios are very sad to watch and, either way, no-one gains.

What can we do to avoid such family breakdown? We can intervene from the start and meet with family members, perhaps a couple of times, so that we can fully understand what has happened to them and what their needs are at this time. This should be helpful for all the family; they will need to talk through all they have been through and how they feel about this. Until they have done this, they will not take in any information we share with them. Meanwhile, we can note who may be particularly vulnerable if the stress continues. Social workers generally do not yet seem to be aware that the theories of working in the aftermath of mass disasters can apply rather well to these traumatized families...

## (2) Necessary Information about the Illness

As we have noted, if families are deprived of this information, then they are *disempowered*. They have no alternative in these circumstances but to learn by trial and error, which is not beneficial for them or for the sufferer. We must give carers a headstart by providing them with a baseline of knowledge which will enable them to achieve necessary expertise and provide a properly supportive network for the recovering sufferer. The sort of information that we might share with them can be found in Chapter 8.

### (3) Explanations About What the Illness Means for the Sufferer

Without these, distrust and hostility may be perpetuated. Few families initially understand enough about delusional thinking and the extent to which delusional thoughts may linger if allowed to fester. Pat's father would have had no chance to rebuild a loving relationship with his daughter without an appreciation of what she had believed about him for so long. In short, the family needs to understand what has been happening to their relative and, it is important to remember, what is happening now. They need to learn how schizophrenia can feel *from within* and to understand how easy it can be to misinterpret the sufferer's behaviour. For example, if they can appreciate the extent of the feelings of apathy and lethargy in this illness, then they are more likely to accept and tolerate behaviour that they might otherwise interpret as idleness. This becomes particularly important when the family can see their relative making splendid progress in some respects and managing to find energy for some things and not others.

### (4) The Role of Medication in this Illness

Most families realize quickly that it is the prescribed drugs which bring the sufferer back to reality. Few are aware that the same drugs have another important role and that is to help prevent further breakdown. Clinical Psychologists in Birmingham found that seventy-five per cent of the relatives in one piece of research they carried out 'possessed little understanding about the function of the medication'.[9] Clearly, families should have this understanding and appreciate that for many sufferers their need for these drugs can be regarded in a similar light to the diabetic sufferer's need for insulin. It is essential that carers have a real understanding of this (together with a knowledge of potential side effects) if they are to help their relative to stay well. They need to know that the sufferers with the most potential to be really well are usually those who are most responsive to the medication, but that these individuals are also the very ones who are most reluctant to keep on taking it. You may remember that Stephen and Tina both discussed this phenomenon in Chapter 5.

## (5) The Potential Risk of Further Breakdown

No-one – but *no-one* – can foresee at the time of a first schizophrenic episode whether or not a sufferer will be prone to relapse. Families need to know this. They need to understand the potential risk of coming off medication and about other factors which can contribute to further breakdown.

## (6) A Lifeline

As everyone agrees that there is no cure for schizophrenia at the present time, then it is essential that sufferers and carers should know how to get help if they need this now or in the future. If we don't provide such a lifeline then we are doing little better than the ostrich which sticks its head in the sand when a problem comes along. If we provide this lifeline then we can avoid delays in 'getting back into the system', while the sufferer becomes more vulnerable.

## (7) The Benefits System and Other Practical Services

Many sufferers will need to use the benefits system at some time, if only to claim sickness benefit during a short illness. Some will have to rely on state benefits indefinitely and families should be guided through the basics of the benefits system so that they can protect sufferers' rights until such time as they are well enough to do this for themselves. In some cases, relatives will need to take on the responsibility for looking after the individual's financial affairs on an ongoing basis and, as many know to their cost, this can be an exhausting process. We will touch on these practical issues in Chapter 8.

Similarly, it is helpful if families can be given an idea of the local mental health facilities which may be appropriate for someone with this illness. So often, sufferers are discharged from hospital after a first episode of schizophrenia without being referred on to one of the various types of resources which could help bring some routine back into their lives. Similarly, families rarely seem to be aware of local sheltered housing projects which might be appropriate for their relative at some time in the future. Too many elderly parents have struggled on for years supporting a sick son or daughter and losing sleep worrying 'what will happen when we're gone?'

## (8) Introduction to Relevant Voluntary Organizations

The benefits to be gained by this are discussed in Chapter 8 and the organizations are listed under 'Useful Addresses' at the end of the book.

## (9) Adequate Information for the Sufferer About the Illness

Regrettably, some sufferers come through a first schizophrenic episode with no idea that their experiences have been due to an illness and remain convinced, therefore, that others are to blame for what has happened to them. Sometimes, of course, they will have a chance to learn the truth at the time of a later breakdown which becomes almost inevitable in these circumstances, but this may be too late. Sometimes, they never achieve this insight; the opportunity to do so has been missed. In Chapter 5 we noted that it is a priority for sufferers that they should gain *insight* into their illness and potential future vulnerability. Ways in which we can meet this vital need are discussed in Chapter 7.

Assuming that we have given families the benefit of these nine services at the time of the initial breakdown, let's now look at how we can meet the priorities for 'life after schizophrenia' highlighted in Chapter 4.

### An End to Denial

Once a sufferer has eventually obtained a diagnosis and appropriate treatment, then there can be no point whatsoever in attempting to deny this later. Doing so can only put the sufferer at risk once again.

The 'revolving door' syndrome is the most pressing problem in psychiatry today and we can only hope to combat this by recognizing that further breakdowns *can be avoided*. This can be achieved if we openly acknowledge that all sufferers are vulnerable to relapse and particularly those who have the most potential to be really well. They are the ones who are so responsive to the anti-psychotic drugs that they become well enough in themselves to feel there is no need to continue with the medication. We can help here by constantly encouraging them to persevere with the medication and by carefully monitoring their progress. We are more likely to succeed in this if we listen to the individuals themselves and to those closest to them.

### Listening and Hearing

Clearly, for a preventive approach such as this to be effective there has to be close liaison between formal and informal carers. In the cases of Jan's son, Mary and Bill's daughter, and John, all of whom had been treated in hospital for a previous breakdown, there was no such liaison. Those closest to diagnosed sufferers were not listened to even when crises were full-blown, let alone when they were developing. In other words, there was no recognition or acknowledgement by the professionals concerned that the families of their clients had any opinions worth listening to or any expertise to offer.

Let us now consider what could have been achieved if they had been prepared to listen.

## Jan's Son

If the psychiatrist had listened to Jan when she first sought her help, then the sufferer and the rest of the family would have been spared an extended period of suffering. After an excellent recovery, this young man had recently made a potentially traumatic move from home and had quickly started to have the hostile ideas about his family which had featured in his illness. All of this, together with his mother's concern, justified an early appointment in which the psychiatrist could have assessed the situation, offered reassurance, arranged extra support as appropriate and adjusted her patient's medication until such time as he settled down again. Instead, nothing was done during the eight weeks before his next scheduled out-patient appointment and then the doctor interpreted his tiredness as signs of his being over-medicated because she was still ignoring Jan's earlier comments.

Again, much later, if hospital ward staff had listened to the young man's own pleas for help and had contacted his psychiatrist before sending him away, they would have discovered that she was by then very anxious to stop the situation getting worse. This sort of 'hit and miss' policy, together with a total lack of effective communication between all parties put the sufferer very much at risk and subjected his family to a living hell for many months. It also eventually put an enormous burden on scarce NHS resources and may well now continue to do so.

## John

As far as John is concerned, his second breakdown started in exactly the same way as his first, demonstrating the importance of the sort of programme carried out at Birmingham in which everyone is alerted to the likely signs of relapse in each individual. If the nature of his first illness had been analyzed, with formal and informal carers noting possible signs of a future relapse, then John's mother would have been listened to when she immediately recognized these signs. Instead, it was a very long time before health professionals listened to her and by then John had broken off relationships with his family and lost both his job and his home. His family are devastated about what has happened. Meanwhile, we have all forfeited the positive contribution that this young man had proved he could make to society. We could have avoided all of these tragedies.

## Mary and Bill's Daughter

As we have noted, in this case an inordinate amount of time was spent doing nothing but listening to this young woman's delusional ideas and in recording these. Meanwhile, the sane but less interesting testimonies of members of her family were ignored. Yet there were five clear pointers on which professionals could and should have focused. These were (1) the testimonies of those closest to her, (2) her past psychiatric history, (3) the fact that she had become ill a couple of months after she stopped taking the medication that had suited her for many years (4) her suddenly disordered lifestyle and (5) her morbid fears about her physical health.

This latter symptom featured in both her and John's first breakdowns and in their relapses. The British Medical Journal has recently drawn attention to this phenomenon in a schizophrenic illness:

> 'Patients with schizophrenia consult (their GP) more often with physical complaints than the average patient, which may divert doctors from reviewing important mental health issues'[10]

In both these cases, focus on this one issue alone could have led to early intervention. Instead, professionals colluded with these young people's delusional ideas. Mary has reported that the experience was chillingly frightening; she describes it this way:

> 'At one point, it seemed that in seeking to protect our daughter and to obtain proper care and treatment for her, we were completely alone in the world. Those who should have been helping us had become the enemy; an enemy who could destroy our family by doing nothing. They did nothing because they had entered our daughter's delusional world and were puppets in the hands of a sick young woman who was unwittingly orchestrating her own destruction'.

Listening to her family and taking a structured approach to this young woman's case could have prevented something which came to resemble a sick comedy. It could also have saved considerable professional time and expense.

## A Professional Responsibility

Unless the professionals involved with each case are determined to get to the bottom of the concerns being reported and then to act upon them, the suffering can go on and on. Worse, as has happened in one of these three cases, things can deteriorate to a tragic level. A structured rather than a 'hit and miss' approach is called for and I believe we should be asking ourselves the following sort of questions each time we work with a case which is new to us and where there is some doubt as to whether the individual is deluded

(1) We know that schizophrenia is not curable at present, so why should I be resistant to the idea that this particular individual might be relapsing?

(2) Why is the family, or other carer, claiming the individual is becoming ill again if this is not the case? What could they possibly have to gain?

(3) What do I know (or can find out) about past episodes in this case that could tend to back up the family's claims?

When the case is eventually resolved or left unresolved, then I believe we should ask ourselves two more questions:

(4) What did I do in my professional capacity to help this individual get on with the rest of his or her life?

(5) What else might I have done which could have minimized further damage to sufferer and family?

One day we may find ourselves more accountable than we are now, with a duty to contribute positively to limiting damage for the individual and minimizing the burden on health care resources. Meanwhile, testing ourselves with these sort of questions each time we respond to pleas for help from families or other carers could more adequately prepare us for the future while also proving conducive to good practice.

## Prompt Reaction

We have looked at the family's need for a prompt reaction and noted that the system is not usually geared to this but that continuity of involvement with the sufferer and carer can help enormously. Bella found this to be essential when she worked as a CPN:

'It is the relatives who usually support the individual in the community and who suffer considerable distress and inconvenience when things go wrong. If you can get them behind you, then I have always found that you can work more effectively with your client. Nine times out of ten I could prevent a relapse by immediately visiting to assess what was happening and by getting hold of the psychiatrist to either call or to review and adjust the medication. This of course is only possible if the doctor also appreciates the need for prompt intervention. This is not always the case, but I and the families I worked with were fortunate in this.'

If community psychiatric nurses can work in this way with the doctor in charge of the sufferer's treatment and care, then there is more chance of quickly getting permission to adjust the individual's dose of medication. In almost all cases, this is what is required at the first signs of a threatened relapse, before the individual starts to lose touch with reality and then refuses this help. This done, the CPN or other involved worker can arrange for extra support to be provided as appropriate at least until the threat of relapse has passed.

**Effective Communication**

We noted earlier that the case of Jan's son was beleaguered with lack of communication at all levels. Heather, who is a nurse manager of a busy outpatient department and also co-ordinator of a local NSF group believes that the majority of complaints in the health service are a direct result of a breakdown of communication. She stresses:

> 'I feel that the very foundation of good care is communication. ALWAYS COMMUNICATE with your colleagues, including GPs, and with carers, clients and anyone else who has a special interest. It can do no harm and can certainly do a power of good!'

Better communication all round would most certainly improve life for sufferers and for families. Carers have already highlighted two examples of the need for this in Chapter 4; the vexed question of over-emphasis on medical confidentiality and the discharge of patients without any recourse to or discussion with the informal carers. Let's take a further look at each of these examples:

*Medical Confidentiality*

Fortunately, undue emphasis on this may be on the decline but there are still some psychiatrists who are adamant about the individual's right to confidentiality. This applies even when it means that the carers are left in the dark about the doctor's treatment plan and the doctor is equally ignorant about their day-to-day experience of the patient's progress. The latter being the case, this, of course, immediately undermines the doctor's ability to look after the patient's welfare properly.

If we look at all closely at the process of surviving this type of illness, one wonders if such doctors are even aware of the enormous potential for their patients to remain well if formal and informal carers work together? Whatever the reason, they cause untold hardship for those trying to do most of the work supporting their patients out in the community and in so doing they put the latter's welfare at risk. Not surprisingly, it is rare to see sufferers flourish in a situation where notions of 'medical confidentiality' take preference over facilitating the 24-hours a day work carried by those trying to provide care for a loved one.

## Discharge of Patients From Hospital Without Recourse to Carers

This was likened to nurses having to take over a shift on a ward without the benefit of a hand-over session. This example should tell us what we need to do for carers before their relative is discharged and this could be the responsibility of any of the staff involved with sufferers during their stay in hospital together with any who will be involved with them back in the community.

In Chapter 4, we saw yet another example of poor communication which comes up all too frequently, this time in the case of Bill's son before the relapse which led to his being imprisoned. This was concerned with his coming off his medication.

## Reduction or Withdrawal of Medication Without Recourse to Carers

Again and again, families and other carers ask that they should be involved in any decision to discontinue or even to reduce the individual's medication. Perhaps discussions in the past few chapters have highlighted the dangers in making such decisions without first checking what is going on with those closest to the sufferer? Those of us who have to pick up the pieces afterwards believe that failure to communicate properly before taking such action contributes more to the 'revolving door' syndrome than any one other factor. Betty is a busy and dedicated CPN who sometimes despairs when a relapse is precipitated by a change in medication which those closest to the individual would never have sanctioned. She points out:

> 'I can't understand this apparent preoccupation with continuously reducing sufferers' medication when this can lead to relapse. There seems to be little recognition of the long uphill struggle that sufferers have had to get well again. The hard work and determination that goes into this should be valued and treasured for what it is. Why can't we *leave well alone* when our clients are beginning to flourish again and remember the maxim "if it ain't broken, don't mend it"?'

## Proper Use of the Law

As we have noted, the Mental Health Act 1983 serves to protect the interests of those individuals who lose touch with reality and their own need for treatment. It also serves to protect the interests of others who may be adversely affected by this. Increasingly, it achieves neither aim. This is not the fault of the legislation itself; it is the fault of those who use it. Every time there is a bid for further legislation, as happened during 1993 – this time from the Secretary of State – all those who regularly oppose it do so on the grounds that the existing law is adequate but that it is not used effectively. They are referring to its provision for sectioning a patient *'in the interests of his health'*. As soon as the debate is ended, there is no further mention of this human failing to use the law properly and nothing changes. Everyone resumes the fantasy that the individual is 'not sectionable' unless he can be shown to be a danger to himself or to others.

Betty finds that her work as a CPN increasingly involves her in trying to persuade colleagues who work with the Mental Health Act to intervene on the part of clients and their families. She is dismayed at the time that passes before anything is done to relieve the suffering and marvels at the burden placed on scarce resources while nothing at all is being achieved.

She has analyzed the handling of some recent cases with which she is familiar and finds the following common features:

(1) Months of suffering after help has been sought from the psychiatric services; for the client, for the family, and in one case for the landlord.

(2) Reluctant acceptance or appreciation of the evidence of carers (despite the fact that involved professionals may reinforce this evidence) until such time as breakdown is complete and obvious.

(3) Delay in initiating a proper assessment as recommended in the Code of Practice[12] before the condition becomes extreme and undeniable.

(4) A series of abortive mental health assessments by various uninformed professionals who claim they saw no evidence of the reported behaviour; that the individual behaved appropriately and was 'not sectionable'.

She says:

'in three cases alone, a total of three years of young people's lives have been wasted by allowing a serious illness to remain untreated. Three families have been driven to despair and they say something like "the people who help are great – the system keeps letting us down".

Three sufferers have been unnecessarily damaged mentally, physically, financially and socially. Two started to improve rapidly once treatment was under way. The third case is still unresolved, with the client having frequent brushes with the police and the family seriously considering moving away from a situation they can no longer tolerate.'

We cannot hope to meet the needs of sufferers and families if we use the mental health legislation in this way. As we noted earlier, everyone concerned claims the Mental Health Act 1983 is adequate but that it is just not used effectively. Until we do something about this, the grim suffering and wastage will continue and this illness will impose an enormous financial burden on our health services. We will return to this subject later and consider how the law should be used if it is to serve the interests of all those affected by this illness.

## CHAPTER 7

# Meeting Needs Identified by Sufferers

We noted in Chapter 5 that sufferers are totally dependent upon others to obtain help for them before their psychosis is acknowledged. Once this is achieved, there is little doubt about their first priority; an urgent urgent need for someone to whom they can turn for reassurance and support.

## A Lifeline

Individuals who have had a schizophrenic breakdown are often most comfortable with 'one-to-one' relationships, but never more so than when their confidence is shattered by a breakdown. This is seemingly not recognized by many of those working with them at that time and it is not unusual for sufferers to be left to themselves while everyone waits for the medication to do its work. Even then, ward staff may still not involve themselves with these patients. Several sufferers discussed this phenomenon at a local NSF group meeting one evening, stressing their unmet need to be able to talk to someone about their experiences while recovering in hospital. A third-year nursing student who attended this meeting suddenly interrupted them to exclaim:

> 'Oh dear, we are told by senior staff to let schizophrenic patients be and to give our time to others on the ward who can be helped.'

She was mortified to learn how misplaced such advice could be and to discover that sufferers could be so articulate and communicate so well. She had learned nothing of value about schizophrenia before that meeting. Bella used to involve students as much as possible in her work with this illness and has commented:

'too many health professionals see schizophrenia as being bad news; few realize how treatable it is and how the cycle of continuing breakdowns can be broken. I have always believed that there would be much more interest in working with this illness if professionals fully appreciated just how treatable it can be.'

Certainly, it does seem that many of those who work with schizophrenia have no real appreciation of the potential in sufferers for understanding what has happened to them and for taking responsibility for their own health, if given the chance. It also seems that these workers have no real understanding of the torment of a psychotic nightmare and a sufferer's natural need for extra support when recovering from this.

Once we discard the idea that constant requests for reassurance are 'attention seeking', we find individuals who are desperate to find a way out of their nightmare and anxious to find someone they can trust enough to share with them their experience and remaining fears. They are in fact *seeking attention* because this is what they need when they are struggling with Sally's 'sense of remoteness' and 'the almost overwhelming 'inner world' of schizophrenia'. The expression 'attention seeking' has unpleasant connotations; *seeking attention* is something we all do if we need this attention and it is not readily available. If this is the case, then perhaps this says rather more about the service we are receiving than about our behaviour?

## A Challenge

However, if we accept the challenge to provide all the attention that individuals recovering from a schizophrenic breakdown so need, then everyone stands to gain. Our patient or client flourishes and our own needs to achieve real job satisfaction are met as well.

Clearly, one person cannot be responsible for the whole reassurance and reality testing programme for any one sufferer. This can be shared, so long as the support is given in a 'one-to-one' situation initially, as discussed in Chapter 5; there is no reason why two or three members of staff should not be involved, with one of these workers playing a key role.

## Reassurance and Reality Testing

The initial purpose of this 'one-to-one' relationship is to provide reassurance. This will be of value only if the worker remains truthful at all times, promoting trust, and avoiding collusion with psychotic ideas. We can indicate respect for such ideas, while providing for the sufferer a much needed hold on reality, with comments such as:

> 'Yes, I understand that this is how it seems to you and I respect that. However, I believe the other patients are just patients; not agents who are out to get you. You are safe now and I think you will soon realize this.'

It should be appreciated that initially the individual will come back over and over again for reassurance; this does not mean we are wasting our time; quite the contrary. These are the tentative beginnings of the acquisition of insight.

## Explanations and Information

We met Heather in Chapter 5. A senior nurse and also the mother of a sufferer, she pleads:

> 'teach our sufferers about their illness and help them to find ways of living around it. Don't deny their condition – teach them how to cope with it and to rule it, rather than it them.'

This has to be sound sense, doesn't it? If we provide explanations for recovering sufferers about what has happened to them and about the illness at this stage in their recovery, then there is every chance that they will gain a healthy insight that will help to protect them throughout the rest of their lives. The sort of information we should share with sufferers includes a detailed coverage of schizophrenic symptoms (see Chapter 2) with further explanations about other aspects of the illness (see Chapter 8 for some ideas).

Falloon and Talbot have described an educational programme they promoted in a hospital in the United States[1] which provided regular seminars for recovering patients on matters such as diagnosis, possible causes and course of the illness and ways of coping with it. Emphasis was given to the role of medication, possible side effects and ways of dealing with these, and finding 'prompts' for remembering to take medication at appropriate times. Relatives were encouraged to join these sessions. This sort of programme can be invaluable, particularly if it is backed up by reassurance and reality-testing with a 'lifeline' worker, as we discussed earlier. I have found that a special kind of groupwork (described in Chapter 12) can also provide an excellent learning situation at the appropriate time and this could aptly complete such a programme.

## Insight

Perhaps we can safely assume that this important matter has been dealt with under the previous headings in this chapter; if we provide the sort of services we have discussed, there should be no need for sufferers to have to struggle on without the benefit of insight into their condition and future vulnerability.

## Changing Attitudes

While everyone working with mental illness agrees that something must be done to change attitudes, there seems to be little understanding that our own 'conspiracy of silence' fuels society's fear of schizophrenia. Lay members of the public learn volumes from our silence, much as sufferers often do, and the subject remains shrouded in mystery and ignorance. This in turn is aggravated by reports in the media of seemingly unprovoked violence and fatalities. Unfortunately good news is seldom 'news'.

All of us working with this illness have a pressing responsibility to spread the good news and help others to understand (1) that schizophrenia is a common illness that happens to ordinary, people, (2) that it is treatable, (3) that most of us have a neighbour or a work colleague or a fellow club member who is a sufferer, but we are probably not aware of this because of the stigma attached to schizophrenia. Yet it is a condition which should, in fact, be acknowledged in much the same way that diabetes is, as both have many similar features.

We do have to change all this if we want to make community care a reality rather than a fiasco. Where do we start? We could start by *communicating*.

## Communicating the Good News

We should take every opportunity we can to talk about schizophrenia with other professionals and workers, especially those working with young people. We should talk with prospective employers, with teenagers in our schools (and some show a real interest in such matters), with young mothers and with local groups who seek guest speakers (and whose members often include someone who wants to come and talk to you quietly afterwards about a relative or friend). We should use the more accessible local media to keep the word schizophrenia 'up front' and familiar, by advertising local events or achievements and by writing articles and letters to the editor each time the illness is in the news; in fact, by thinking positive and acting on this at every opportunity.

Most important of all, we should encourage and enable articulate survivors, who want to do this, to take part in educational programmes and meetings of all kinds. This illness, like everything else, becomes more acceptable when it is seen to be associated with individuals with whom most people are happy to identify.

## Communication With Sufferers

The first priority for sufferers is that we should start to *communicate* with them from the moment we have contact with them. As we have seen, this does not usually happen, despite the clear need for it. Perhaps we can better see how important this communication is if we remember we are using it to reach out to someone who is very ill, offering a lifeline.

This achieved, then perhaps the phrase 'thinking positive' under the previous heading, is the all-important one when it comes to communicating with the victims of this illness. We really must try to communicate to them our positive feelings about them and about their diagnosis. This latter may seem unlikely on the face of it, but there is really no reason at all why we shouldn't have positive feelings about one of the few really treatable mental illnesses. Most of us in the caring professions feel dejected when we can do little or nothing for any of our clients. This need not be the case with schizophrenia; the more *proactive* we are and the sooner we intervene, the greater the chance that we can do something of lasting value and really influence the quality of the individual's life.

## An Appreciation of the Role of the Medication

As Stephen and Tina demonstrated in Chapter 5 in their papers on this aspect of their treatment, coming to terms with the need to take anti-psychotic drugs, perhaps indefinitely, can be the turning point in a sufferer's recovery. Tina feels that the importance of this is no longer appreciated by some professionals and has asked me to note her concern that:

> 'Nowadays, the modern approach by some professionals seems to rely on little or even no medication at all and a lot of the treatment is "talking therapy" and all sorts of groupwork. This is fine for a little while, but what happens when the therapy ends? Not only have you got no groupwork, you have no back-up most of the time and you have no medication. And I believe that's when the nightmare begins yet again. I feel so worried for new young sufferers coming along now...'

Tina has reason to be concerned about this trend because although she has a caring and knowledgeable psychiatrist, other professionals have encouraged her to come off medication, as someone as articulate and capable as herself should be able to be strong and cope without 'this crutch'. Comments like this can be lethal, in view of the innate reluctance of sufferers to take medication and because of the frailty of their self-image. We should focus on congratulating them on their courage and determination finally to accept the need for their medication if they are to be free to get on with the rest of their lives.

Bella, who started her nursing career back in the early 1950s before the anti-psychotic medication was available, commented recently:

> 'I have always tried to impress on my colleagues and on students that if they had seen schizophrenia before we had medication they would have no doubts about the effectiveness of these drugs. If you take illnesses such as heart-disease, epilepsy and diabetes, people suffering with these conditions can remain well provided the environment is right, their general health is good and they have their medication. Exactly the same can be said for schizophrenia. The anti-psychotic drugs are certainly no more dangerous than many in daily use for other conditions and we know that they not only relieve the symptoms of a schizophrenic breakdown but also help to prevent further relapses, which can certainly cause irreversible damage.'

She worries, as Tina does, that there is ambivalence towards drug treatment now and although she appreciates that doctors have to try to find a balance between the risks of further breakdown and the risks of possible long-term undesirable side effects from the drugs, Bella has the same concerns as those discussed by Betty in the last chapter:

> 'some doctors aim to continuously decrease the dosage of the medication taken by their patients rather than stopping at the point where the sufferer is clearly doing very well. The trouble with this is that if the blood levels of the drug become too low, patients can become ill too suddenly for us to prevent a breakdown. Ironically, their breakdown then has to be treated with very high doses of the same or a similar drug!'

I believe this comment of Bella's takes us back to her earlier one in which she regrets the fact that many health professionals see schizophrenia as 'bad news'. If we are ambivalent about the prognosis in this illness and if we are ambivalent about the treatments we use, then we can set up a self-fulfilling prophecy in which sufferers are at best never quite well enough to free themselves from dependence on ourselves and at worst will relapse yet again and fuel the 'revolving door' syndrome.

Continued research findings over the past few decades confirm that there is a considerably higher risk of relapse if the anti-psychotic drugs are discontinued[2] and Richard Wyatt's paper 'Neuroleptics and the Natural Course of Schizophrenia' concludes:

'The concept that initial psychosis and later relapses might have long-term effects on morbidity suggests that greater consideration should be given to the usual clinical practice of taking patients off neuroleptics after they have recovered from an acute psychosis and appear stable'[3]

Well recovered sufferers whom my colleagues and I have worked with over the years have all stressed the importance of continuing to take medication for this illness. Several of them have contributed to this book. Sally insists that after decades of being ill, it was only when she was eventually prescribed anti-psychotic medication that she started to get well. Furthermore, it was only when she learned to have respect for this medication that she finally managed 'to stay on the right side of the tracks', as she puts it. If we are to help as many sufferers as possible resume a normal lifestyle, then I believe we should take notice of the experiences of those who have gained insight into their illness and have learned how to protect themselves from further relapse. If they and other potentially well sufferers can overcome their reluctance to take medication, surely they have the right to expect us to recognize and support them in their triumph over this devastating illness?

## Respect for the Family Unit

Our approach to a family in crisis, or threatened by crisis, should always be shaped by a sound appreciation that the sufferer is part of that unit and usually wants to remain so. If we do this, we can avoid comments of the kind I have heard too often over the years, such as 'Well, you'd be paranoid if you had to live with those parents!' When applied to the long-suffering elderly parents of a forty-five-year-old man who refuses to live with anyone other than them and who also frequently declines to take his medication, this sort of remark is really not worthy of 'caring professionals'. As Pat has reminded us in Chapter 5, sufferers and families are not living together because they hate each other; their cause is usually one and the same.

It is at troubled times like this that Sally wants us to give families 'the means with which to cope'. It is at times like this that professionals can give families the support that will enable them to 'soldier on'. It is at times like this that lack of support and judgmental attitudes can be the last straw for a family that has suffered one too many trauma.

We should bear in mind that the family is a unit and that it is inappropriate to 'take sides' and to collude with psychotic delusions. While I have been writing this chapter, one sufferer has told me about the delusional ideas of his very recent breakdown, finishing with, 'Well I know what made me believe the crazy things I said, but what was *their* excuse?' The young man was referring to the professionals who chose to believe his ravings rather than listen to what his family were saying. We have noted that sometimes professionals are ambivalent about drug treatment for schizophrenia. Sometimes they may even be ambivalent about the illness itself, to the point that they can 'take aboard really mad ideas' (I quote this same young man) rather than acknowledge its presence. Perhaps they should not be surprised that sufferers are neither flattered nor impressed by this.

## After Out-patient Clinics?

Returning to the question of continuity of supervision in the community, it seems quite possible that out-patient clinics will soon be seen to be a relic of the old hospital system rather than a part of community care. It may be that there will be opportunities for change. If so, perhaps psychiatrists based in the community could be freed to deal with threatened emergencies *when they occur*, to be available at resource centres on a 'drop in' basis (with screening to prevent wasting of their time) and to be available for inevitable requests from CPNs to monitor their patients' medication or to sanction a temporary adjustment to this while they still agree to this, before the psychosis sets in.

Similarly, when it comes to the provision of training for new doctors, they could profit from visiting patients and their families in their homes with CPNs and other workers in the community. This would provide opportunities for learning about the everyday problems of sufferers and also for accompanying colleagues to potential crisis situations when these threatened. It is certain that they would learn more about this illness from this sort of experience than from a series of short structured interviews provided by the out-patient clinic system. Although some recovered sufferers, particularly those working and out of touch with other mental health services, might not be covered by such arrangements, they could write seeking an appointment with the psychiatrist – the doctor who knows them – when they felt the need for this, keeping in touch with their GP in the meantime. Any emergency could be dealt with in the same way that it would be now if this occurred between out-patient appointments.

Perhaps this would be a more effective way of working with this illness. Experience demonstrates that interviews are notoriously inadequate tools when it comes to assessing the vulnerability of schizophrenia sufferers; the very ones whom we need to monitor if they are to be protected from relapse.

### Equal Opportunities for Employment

As we noted in Chapter 5, if sufferers disclose their medical history, there is little chance they will get an interview for a job, however well they may be qualified for it. Short of legislation to deal with this discrimination, it is difficult to see how it can change, particularly in an age where under-employment is likely to be the rule. I have argued earlier (and elsewhere[4]) that if employers do not need to know about 'spent' criminal records, then they should not need to know about a mental illness which may not have caused any problem for decades. Employers can make use of other existing safeguards such as seeking reliable references, the use of introductory probationary periods and a check on sick leave days during any recent employment.

Meanwhile, those of us who work with able sufferers who are desperate to find rewarding work can perhaps help them first to find voluntary work – preferably something worthy of their ability – and gradually earn a reputation for themselves and references which may come in useful. Alternatively, they can try taking on temporary work with an agency. This can provide some experience and a chance to 'pace' one's introduction back to the workplace. It can also lead to an employer asking the 'temp' to stay on permanently because the individual seems right for the job. Some employers prefer to recruit suitable staff this way and often decline to seek background information on the new employee. Similarly, jobs without pensions are easier to obtain than careers tied up with this sort of long-term benefit, for the sort of reasons discussed in Chapter 5. I have found that some individuals have benefited from one or other of these kinds of approach to getting work but many still remain frustrated in their efforts. Naomi Smith, a nurse for many years, has commented wryly:

> 'Now, if I am asked, I advise my schizophrenic friends not always to admit that they have or have had this diagnosis. Our society does not always deserve to be told the truth'.[4]

She has a point.

### An End to all Discrimination

Individuals who have had a psychotic illness face discrimination in areas other than employment. They have problems obtaining visas and very little, if any, hope of emigrating. They have difficulty obtaining insurance cover of all kinds, paying well over the odds if they achieve this. They are unlikely to be accepted as adoptive or foster parents. They can have trouble finding accommodation and keeping a doctor. All in all, it is no wonder that sufferers seek to deny a diagnosis which brings with it 'third class citizen' status. What can we do about this 'deterrent policy'? I believe we can make headway with this only by concentrating on changing attitudes. Some of my clients have demonstrated their value to society once given the opportunity to do so; they make excellent ambassadors if we can only help them open some doors.

## Quality of Life

Now we come to the practical and basic everyday issues that are so important for most of us but not necessarily attainable by sufferers. For some of them, achieving these basic needs will depend to a greater or lesser extent on the help and guidance they receive from health professionals and other workers in the community. Let's look at each in turn.

### (1) Satisfactory Level of Income

If sufferers cannot work for a living on a permanent basis, then they probably need to claim state benefits. Anyone who has any experience with the benefits system will know that this is so complex that it can intimidate the most healthy and able in our society. For those who are undermined by an illness that robs them of motivation and staying power, the long waits in DSS offices, the filling in of reams of forms requiring answers to seemingly irrelevant and unintelligible questions can be a deterrent to claiming their rights. Those of us who work with this illness should be very careful to encourage any isolated sufferers not to give up the struggle to claim the benefits due to them. They will need help through this maze if they are not to give up (and so drop out of the system). To a lesser extent, those with families will also need help, initially at least, and whenever the individual's status changes. This essential work is often neglected and many sufferers are not receiving their full entitlements. This matter is discussed more fully in Chapter 8.

Having said that, I wish that a duty to provide bus passes to individuals on benefits because of a mental illness could be imposed on all local authorities. Sufferers in at least one London borough certainly achieve a better quality of life because they are allocated bus and train passes which allow them to take advantage of free or cheap facilities which would otherwise be beyond their means because of the cost of travel.

### (2) Satisfactory Accommodation

If the sufferer does not have an option of living with relatives, then finding the right accommodation becomes a priority. It is my experience that very few individuals who are prone to the sort of symptoms associated with schizophrenia should live on their own. These symptoms tend to return if the individual has nothing to do and nothing else to focus on. Only a minority of sufferers seem to thrive on living on their own. Most complain sadly of loneliness and not wanting to return to their bedsits or flatlets after being in the company of other people. Some live in squalor, not because this is what they want but because they cannot relate to their isolated 'home' or bear to be there except to sleep. Equally deprived are those who stay in bed all day because there is no-one to urge them out of it.

I have quoted before a letter from one sufferer, describing his ideal accommodation:

> 'A bed-sitting room with adjoining kitchen and bathroom, with a communal sitting-room... where one good meal a day is served, to be situated in a house with about eight other people residing... the people to be carefully selected so that all are compatible, the house to be in a quiet locale near the town centre, with a visiting nurse or doctor once a week.'[5]

This model is very similar to the one that sufferers discuss with myself and my colleagues. Each individual can have independence and privacy but need never be alone unless this is desired. A less supportive version of this model would suit many individuals who are quite capable of cooking for themselves. Where this would not be the case, then the provision of 'one good meal a day' would mean that someone would be available to check that each tenant was eating well and to seek help if there was any cause for concern; a daily monitoring that would lessen the workload of busy professionals in the community.

## (3) Rewarding and Stimulating Occupation

Again, unless sufferers are doing voluntary or paid work which suits them, then they may be dependent to a greater or lesser extent on day care resources for stimulation. One such example which may effectively meet this need is discussed in Chapter 10.

It is regrettable that even the right to do voluntary work is becoming a luxury nowadays for many sufferers as the benefits system has clamped down on claimants doing more than a few hours each week — for reasons scarcely aimed at improving the quality of life for individuals keen to help themselves and others.

## (4) Supportive Social Network

This book deals in detail with the most important part of this network; that is with families and how to give them 'the means with which to cope' so that they can provide the support that the sufferer needs. For many individuals another important part of this network is provided by their peers. My colleagues and I have been impressed by the quality of relationships which have been formed by sufferers we know. Some of these have provided a social network which some 'normal' young people might well envy. This does not just happen. It first needs nurturing, but the results are exciting and well worth the effort; a tribute, in fact, to the caring and mutual support shared by so many who have had this illness. For those who lack any real family support, this social network can provide a sense of belonging and means of achieving some real quality of life. For those who are more fortunate, it is a bonus and one that is touched on again later.

### Damage Limitation

When all is said and done, the main priority for every individual who falls victim to schizophrenia, is *damage limitation* in a treatable illness. We can only contribute to this damage limitation if we intervene sooner rather than later, if we share our knowledge and expertise and if we help to prevent further relapses, 'which can certainly cause irreversible damage' as Bella has commented earlier. As the World Health Organization found in 1979:

> 'Admission to hospital is often a source of considerable and protracted disruption and stress for all parties and relapse can exacerbate social and psychological impairments associated with the disorder as well as further increasing an individual's vulnerability to relapse.'[6]

In Chapter 3, we looked at what happened to Malcolm and his family when he developed a schizophrenic illness and said we would come back to this later. His is a tragic example of a case where the principles of damage limitation were ignored. At what stages in this tragedy should professionals have intervened?

### Post Mortem

(1) When Malcolm was admitted to hospital several months after his problems began there were already clear signs that something was very wrong. The psychiatrist did not check out the evidence by finding out what had been causing the family so much concern. Malcolm was observed in hospital and those observing also

listened to his protests that he needed 'more space' and a chance to be independent. They seemingly decided his problems originated in his parents, and their attitude to him, and this was the message which came through in the family sessions.

(2) Malcolm dodged the family sessions by leaving during the first one and never returning. The therapists did not follow this up. The parents' experience of these sessions demonstrated that the 'official view' was that *they* were at fault. The therapists did not hear what the parents were saying about their continuing experience with Malcolm. What was the purpose of these sessions?

(3) Malcolm refused to go to his 'out-patient' appointments. Nothing was done about this, in the same way as nothing was done about his opting out of the family sessions.

(4) The GP, who had intervened very promptly in the first instance, now declared herself unable to help further because Malcolm was avoiding her and the psychiatric team. Another opportunity for follow-up was missed; she could have sought a domiciliary visit from the psychiatrist concerned.

(5) When Malcolm threatened his mother, holding a bread knife to her throat, the doctor and social worker who came to assess him could have sectioned him on two of the three grounds for formal admission (see Chapter 8 for these), so that he could not discharge himself before effective help was at hand. They had ample evidence of his previous lack of co-operation which made it likely he would do just what he did do; he would vote with his feet.

(6) From this point on, professionals referred to Malcolm's 'bad' behaviour and started to put the onus on the parents to be strong and not put up with this. We have seen how untreated schizophrenic symptoms are likely to lead to behaviour which can then be judged 'bad' rather than 'mad'.

(7) When Malcolm attacked his mother (because he was feeling threatened by the pressure to see the psychiatrist again) and blackened her eye, the GP had more than enough evidence to recommend that Malcolm should be sectioned, again on two of the grounds for formal admission. Instead, telling his mother that she didn't have to put up with this sort of behaviour once more put the onus on the family to do something and, seemingly, throw him out.

(8) Even when the parents did just that because they did not know what else to do, Malcolm was still given no help other than the finding of the first of many lodgings over the next twenty months. During this long period there was plenty of evidence that landladies could no more cope with him than his parents could. It was also evident that the young man was looking increasingly unwell. However, because he had been labelled 'bad' not 'mad' by themselves, professionals felt able to keep on turning away. The only exception to this rule was the police. The family have nothing but gratitude and praise for their help during this nightmare few years but they too were unable to persuade health professionals that Malcolm was ill.

Did *you* wonder why the professionals concerned did not intervene for Malcolm on this sort of occasion? Would you have been happy to look back on this case if you had been one of the professionals involved? It is difficult to conclude that any of those who were trained and paid to provide care or treatment for a sick young person took any responsibility for ensuring this was provided for Malcolm. In no way did they protect him or his family from the potential ravages of an untreated psychosis. They first of all decided that the problem was caused by the parents; *their* behaviour was at fault. Later, when the professionals involved found themselves no more able to cope with Malcolm than his parents, the official view changed to the problem being caused by Malcolm himself; *his* behaviour was at fault. Unfortunately, the responsibility for doing something about it was left to the parents either way.

Sometimes there is evidence of a disturbing lack of mercy in our approach to schizophrenia. I hope those who choose to blame the victims of this illness for their own predicament, and then turn away, do so because they don't know what else to do. I hope this is the case, because something can be done about these feelings of impotence. I hope too that this book can contribute to replacing such feelings with confidence and a determination to limit the damage done to these individuals. By doing this, it could also contribute to enormous savings of scarce resources which now have to be provided for Malcolm and others like him who have become seriously disabled whilst waiting for acknowledgement of their illness. In the meantime, perhaps we should heed Heather's comments on difficult cases like Malcolm's:

'Never *reject* and never expect a family to do so either. This goes against all the natural instincts of motherhood and family ties. Other ways *must* be found of helping the family to cope. If you feel that all avenues have been exhausted, call a case conference and invite all interested parties, have a brainstorming session and then TRY AGAIN!'

In case this might seem like 'pie in the sky', Heather goes on to illustrate her point with a case she became involved in during 1988, when wearing her NSF co-ordinator's 'hat':

'I was contacted by a carer whose only son, now in his thirties, had been displaying signs of mental health problems since his teenage years. He was prone to sudden outbursts of destructive anger (literally smashing up the home – furniture, windows, doors, etc) which he could not explain and always regretted. His mother had been advised to take out a court injunction against him and call the police if he tried to contact her. In desperation, she did this and he spent six weeks in prison. Fortunately, she contacted the local NSF group at the same time and we worked together to find a more satisfactory solution.

I managed to gain the son's confidence and persuaded him to seek help for himself from the mental health team. Since there is no self-referral system locally, this involved many visits to the GP which the son found very stressful. However, a member of the mental health team finally and reluctantly agreed to see him and he was started on depot injections. This had a manifold benefit in that it evened out his tremendous mood swings and prevented the unwanted outbursts of agitation and anger. It also stopped his continual overdosing with oral medication in a useless effort to gain some calm in his life and it enable him and his mother to start to rebuild their relationship and for him to be accepted back into the family home.

He is a very likeable and caring person and yet he had been totally rejected by the statutory services; in fact I had been strongly advised by a senior member of the mental health team to stay well away from this person as he was a "thoroughly bad lot".'

The problem with the 'bad' not 'mad' syndrome is that it so often proves very responsive to anti-psychotic medication! This in turn suggests we have a pressing responsibility to persevere until we find a solution; we do not have the right to reject.

In the last four chapters we have highlighted many of the expressed needs of sufferers and carers and looked at ways that we can go about attempting to meet these needs. The rest of the book is concerned with identifying and sharing tools which can help us to do this.

# III
# A Needs Based Approach

## CHAPTER 8

# Explanations and Sharing Information

It is quite possible that the most useful thing that all of those working with schizophrenia can do for families is to share the available knowledge on this illness with them. This can be done in various ways but perhaps the best approach is to provide some sort of 'user friendly' guide, or series of papers, which can preferably be backed up by training sessions which allow for discussion on each topic in turn. Ideally, the guide would include the following basic information:

(1) Schizophrenia

(2) Its incidence

(3) Its symptoms

(4) The likely course of the illness

(5) The role of medication

(6) Understanding and Support

(7) Factors that help and hinder recovery

(8) Mental Health law

(9) State Benefits

(10) The voluntary sector.

Let's take a look at each of these items in turn and at the sort of information we might provide if we want those reading it to gain an understanding of the basics of the illness:

## (1) Schizophrenia

Schizophrenia is a serious illness which usually attacks young people in the prime of life. It is a psychosis, which means that its victims can lose touch with reality. When this happens they do not appreciate that they are ill and so they refuse treatment. This is an illness in which one's perception, thoughts and emotions become distorted and disturbed. Schizophrenia is not a 'split personality' nor is it particularly associated with violence. In fact, individuals with this illness tend to be rather timid and reserved. Although schizophrenia can wreak havoc with its victims' lives, there is another side to the coin; a good proportion of sufferers tend to enjoy youthful good looks which belie their chronological age. This illness also seems to favour an above average number of talented individuals with sometimes outstanding intellectual or artistic flair. Similarly, a significant minority of sufferers score notable athletic and sporting triumphs before the illness strikes.

### What causes Schizophrenia?

No-one really knows. We suspect that schizophrenia is a group of illnesses with a classic cluster of symptoms which may originate from several different causes.

Around half of all cases of schizophrenia run in families; we don't know why some family members become ill and others don't. Neither do we know what causes all those cases of schizophrenia which don't run in families. Research over the past five years indicates that something may go wrong during pregnancy or around the birth of the individual.

It seems that there is some sort of malfunctioning within the brain in this illness. This may be connected with 'nerve messengers' known as neurotransmitters and one of these – *dopamine* – is directly affected by the main drugs prescribed for schizophrenia. Ideas in the 1960s and 1970s that faulty upbringing caused it have been completely discredited; families are not to blame for schizophrenia.

### 'Trigger' Factors Which May Pre-empt Breakdown

Certain factors frequently feature in the immediate recent history of newly diagnosed sufferers and these are

(1) **hormone upheaval;** most first episodes of schizophrenia in women take place after puberty, childbirth, or, less frequently, menopause. Most first episodes in men take place just after puberty.

(2) **recovery from a virus;** it is quite common for a first episode of schizophrenia to follow a bout of influenza, for example.

(3) **a move away from home and family;** so often those closest to relatives cannot describe the actual breakdown because sufferers were away from home, making them more vulnerable.

(4) **use of street drugs;** increasingly it is common to find new sufferers who have been abusing drugs such as LSD, amphetamines or, more often, cannabis. Sometimes this has been a social habit but it may also reflect a need to 'self-medicate' and so escape from unwelcome symptoms. There is a serious question-mark over the use of such drugs for some vulnerable individuals.

## (2) The Incidence of Schizophrenia

Despite the secrecy surrounding it, schizophrenia is a very common illness. One in every one hundred of us worldwide can expect to have a schizophrenic episode at some time in our life; however, the chances decline with age as eighty per cent of all cases will be diagnosed between the ages of sixteen and twenty-five years. Although the incidence of schizophrenia is divided equally between women and men, the latter usually develop it at a younger age and tend to be more seriously affected in the long term.

Although just under a half of all cases run in families, most sufferers are born to parents without this diagnosis. Anyone with a blood relative with schizophrenia has a greater risk than the rest of the population, that is,

> With an uncle, aunt, niece or first cousin, the risk is raised to 2–3 per cent. With one parent, brother or sister, the risk is raised to 10 per cent. With two parents, the risk is raised to 40 per cent. With an identical twin, the risk is raised to 47 per cent.

The case of identical twins, who share exactly the same genes, points to a greatly enhanced risk for the well twin but also to other factors influencing the more or less equal odds that this individual will stay well. Recent research has suggested that the individual who becomes schizophrenic may be disadvantaged at birth, being smaller and generally thriving less well than its twin.

Many people affected by this illness want to know whether or not they should have children. In our present state of knowledge, we might advise them that their everyday health and their ability to cope with the inevitable stress and responsibilities of child-rearing is probably a more important consideration than any genetic risk.

## (3) Symptoms

These depend on whether sufferers have the acute form of the illness or the chronic form. Acute schizophrenia is characterized by all the bizarre experiences we associate with a nervous breakdown. These may be divided into three main types:

### (i) Altered Perception

The individual's senses of sight, hearing, touch, taste and smell may all be affected; they can become ultra sensitive and/or alter the individual's perception of what is happening around them. One common example of this phenomenon is the hearing of 'voices' which are very real for the sufferer. One type of 'voice' is often commanding and bullying, another type may give a running commentary of everything the individual is doing. Perhaps most upsetting of all, a third type of voice may seem to belong to a loved one, thus seriously threatening a valued relationship unless both parties know what is happening.

### (ii) Disturbed Thought Processes

These can include feelings that one's thoughts have taken on a life of their own, flitting from one thing to another, or that they are being controlled by an outside source.

### (iii) Delusional Ideas

These can best be described as fixations which are very definitely impervious to reason; it is important to understand this. The best known are paranoid delusions and delusions of grandeur because they are used in everyday language but there are many others. Significantly, the experiences in (i) and (ii) can contribute to these delusional ideas.

These are just a few of the phenomena we call 'positive' symptoms because they add something (albeit unwelcome) to the individual's experience. On the other hand the 'negative' symptoms of the chronic form of the illness take something away, seemingly changing and draining the personality. These symptoms include an undermining apathy and lethargy, a blunting of the emotions, problems with initiating a conversation or engaging in 'small talk', and withdrawal into oneself. Sometimes these sort of symptoms can feature in the aftermath of an acute breakdown, but if they persist then the sufferer has probably slipped into the chronic form of the illness.

A particularly trying symptom which can feature in both types of schizophrenia is the 'turning night into day syndrome'. This upturning of the body's normal 24-hour clock can result in sufferers coming to life late in the evening and eventually falling asleep not long before the rest of the world arises.

## (4) The Course of the Illness

Sufferers may be divided into four groups for the purpose of indicating the sort of prognosis associated with a schizophrenic illness:

(i)   Around 25 per cent who may have no more than one breakdown. They may experience residual symptoms and may need to take medication indefinitely to avoid relapse.

(ii)  Those who have intermittent breakdowns, some of whom will keep well between these and some of whom will be seen to gradually deteriorate after each relapse.

(iii) Those who become chronically ill; whose 'negative' symptoms persist, with possible irreversible damage. This involves a detrimental change in personality and social functioning. Sufferers may still remain at risk from further acute relapses.

(iv)  Around 10 per cent of all sufferers who will need ongoing intensive care because of the severity of their illness and who may suffer from either the acute or the chronic form of schizophrenia.

It is important to note that all the potentially well individuals in groups (i) and (ii) remain at risk of potential damage inflicted by further breakdown, demonstrating how much the course of this illness can be affected by the avoiding of any threatened relapse.

## (5) Medication

In schizophrenia, the role of medication is two-fold. First, it is the only means by which we can rescue someone from a schizophrenic breakdown. Second, it can help to prevent further relapse if taken regularly at a level which enables the individual to function well; this in itself can take up to several years to achieve in some cases. Sufferers may refuse to take medication for two reasons; (i) because of troublesome side effects and (ii) because they do not believe they have an illness. If it is for the first reason, then advice should be sought from those supervising the individual's treatment. If it is for the second, then every effort should be made to win the sufferer's trust and co-operation the next time round, if it is too late this time.

## About the Medication

The first medication to help relieve the symptoms of this illness was discovered by accident in the early 1950s. Largactil and various similar drugs which followed have changed the face of the world for people with this illness. One of their main functions is to combat a seeming excess of dopamine available in the brains of sufferers experiencing the 'positive' symptoms of this illness. However, it turns out that there is no simple equation such as *schizophrenia = excess available dopamine* and we don't know if the latter is a cause or effect of the illness. More recent drugs have focused on the functioning of other neurotransmitters as well as dopamine and it seems that these are helping some of those sufferers who have not responded to the original drugs.

Neuroleptic drugs can be prescribed orally on a day-to-day basis and/or by depot injection, on a fortnightly, three-weekly, or monthly basis. Some sufferers are loathe to try injections but they do have some very real advantages: (1) the distribution of the drug is more controlled, (2) they do away with the bother of remembering, or in some cases even deciding, to take tablets several times a day, and (3) professionals can more successfully monitor the individual's drug treatment.

## About Side Effects

Some sufferers have troublesome side effects with these drugs; these may include weight gain, muscle stiffness, dry mouth, tremor and restlessness. They may include less tangible effects such as bouts of excessive tiredness (which may also be caused by the illness) or feelings that the medication makes one feel 'different' and changed in some way. Most of these unwanted effects can be treated by one of several 'side effect' drugs which can usually be tapered off after a while. Although it is not a good idea to take 'side effect' medication unless there is a specific need for this, some individuals can have a quite violent 'lock-jaw' type reaction to initial doses of a neuroleptic drug so it is worth asking the doctor for a prescription for the anti-dote medication 'just in case'. Some individuals do continue to have some unwanted side effects, as is the case with every type of medicine, but careful monitoring and adjustment can resolve many of these problems.

## More Serious Side Effects

There has been much adverse publicity about the risk of one serious side effect of these drugs; tardive dyskinesia. This unpleasant condition manifests itself as an involuntary twitching of the facial muscles and is difficult to treat successfully. It is claimed that it is associated with long-term neuroleptic drug treatment but it should be noted that it was recognized before the discovery of this medication and is still seen in elderly individuals who have never been treated. Also tardive dyskinesia is not something that I or several of my long-term serving colleagues have seen at all often. Neverthelesss, it is a real cause of concern and may be the main reason for some doctors' emphasis on minimizing the prescribed dose of medication. There is, however, no evidence that this will lessen any risk.

As we have noted, several rather different drugs became available in the early 1990s which focus particularly on neurotransmitters other than dopamine. It seems that at least two of these can have potentially fatal effects for some individuals, so all those using them have to be monitored carefully by regular blood tests. One of these – Clozaril – was withdrawn from the market when the potential risks became known but it has gradually been re-introduced under rigid controls and careful supervision because of the need to find effective drugs for those who are not helped by the original drugs.

## (6) Understanding and Support

Medication has the most important role to play in a sufferer's recovery and in staying well, but the support of the family runs it a close second. To be really effective, this support will rely on having a real understanding of 'schizophrenia from within' and this will be expedited by the sort of information provided in this guide, backed up by discussion and further reading. Ideally, professionals looking after the sufferer will also help families to understand how the symptoms have affected their relative and how these might in turn affect their relationships with those closest to them. Meanwhile, a good start can be achieved by families if they consider a few golden rules:

### (i) Try to Accept What Has Happened

Avoid the temptation to contrast previous with present potential. Some parents and spouses are faced with the need to adjust their sights when offspring or partner may no longer fulfil former ambitions or career potential

This is probably the saddest and most difficult adjustment which families have to make; how much worse this must be for the sufferer...

Similarly, try to resist the temptation to be critical when the sufferer lacks motivation and shows no incentive; any improvements will be achieved by positive and gentle encouragement rather than by criticism, which may just further bruise a damaged self-esteem.

### (ii) Recognize That Schizophrenia is an Illness

Give your relative the dignity of a 'sick' role. This does not imply any need to pamper or indulge; it implies understanding and respect. It also helps to put into context certain traits common to most of us when we are not well when we tend to become rather demanding, with an apparent disregard at times for others' needs. Similarly, it explains the need for any clinging behaviour that is causing concern; until sufferers start to feel well and confident again, they tend to use one person as a lifeline and this is often the mother. Instead of worrying about this, it may be a good idea to use this relationship to persuade your relative to go out for a walk with you, or join you on a shopping trip or at a night-school class.

### (iii) Look After the Carer

Remember how important *you* are both as a support to someone who needs you and as a person in your own right. Get all the help you can from those working with this illness and then just do your best. Pause sometimes and give yourself a hug; remember, what you are doing is invaluable and the medals may not be handed out in this life!

### (7) Factors That Help and Hinder Recovery

There are several factors that can help expedite and maintain a good recovery; persevering with medication, having enough stimulation, developing a routine and healthy lifestyle and, of course, shouting for help if there is cause for concern.

### (i) Medication

It is important to persevere with the medication and to resist all attempts to reduce this too far just because the sufferer is 'doing well'. If so, that's great and it's highly unlikely to be the case that he or she is over-medicated.

## (ii) Stimulation and Periods of Rest

It is important that recovering sufferers have enough stimulation to offset the undermining apathy and lethargy of the illness.

Stimulation can be provided by making use of any leisure facilities which might attract the sufferer, particularly if a family member or friend joins in. It can also be provided by sessions at a day care resource or local college, or by doing a few hours voluntary work or by taking part in frequent outings with the family.

These activities may need to be interspersed with short periods of rest, much the same as if the individual were recovering from a serious physical illness. What should be avoided is lingering in bed for hours on end as this sort of inactivity will breed inactivity and even deterioration.

## (iii) Developing a Routine

This is important and should be attempted sooner rather than later. It can begin with becoming used to getting up at a suitable time (remember, this may be later than average if the individual tends to be awake most of the night), and taking an interest in washing, dressing and making a fuss of oneself. Some sufferers find it very tempting not to bother with their appearance and hygiene because of feelings of lethargy. This modest but positive start to the day, together with a series of regular activities during the week, can gradually lead to an acceptable routine which will in turn expedite recovery.

## (iv) A Healthy Lifestyle

A healthy wholefood diet can help combat feelings of lethargy, particularly if the main emphasis in the diet is on fruit, vegetables and protein rather than starch. This emphasis can help offset cravings in this illness for stodgy and sweet foods and also the weight-gain which can be a side-effect of the medication. Similarly, many sufferers definitely benefit from exercise such as a fairly brisk walk or short bouts of more energetic activity. Adopting a daily routine which includes (1) regular times for regular getting up and going to bed, (2) regular whole meals which minimize the intake of stodgy and processed foods and (3) some moderate exercise each day, will do much to 'normalize' a sufferer's everyday life.

## (v) Being Alert to Early Signs of Relapse

Be aware that there can always be a risk of relapse and do not hesitate to ask for advice if you are worried about any change in your relative, carefully explaining the reason for your concern.

Some of the factors that can hinder recovery and maintaining that recovery may be beyond the control of the sufferer, such as physical stress and unwelcome changes, but others will not be:

### (a) ALCOHOL AND DRUG ABUSE

Heavy alcohol consumption is not helpful in this illness and the continuing use of street drugs such as cannabis seems to eliminate any chance of successful treatment. It is worth noting, however, that former abusers sometimes take up either or both types of abuse again when their drug treatment is withdrawn or reduced too far. If this seems to be happening, then it is important to point this out to the supervising doctor.

### (b) CHANGE AND TOO MUCH EXCITEMENT

Many of us don't like change but this is particularly true of some sufferers who find it very threatening. They may even refuse to move away from their home district with parents they have previously clung to. Similarly, too much excitement, however pleasurable this may seem to them at the time, can make some sufferers vulnerable.

### (c) PHYSICAL STRESSES

These can put the individual at risk and can include the aftermath of an attack of influenza, the need for major surgery, or the sort of hormonal upheaval such as that follows childbirth. Special care should be taken at times when sufferers have to cope with these sort of risk factors.

## (8) Mental Health Law

This allows for the sectioning under the Mental Health Act 1983 of someone who is too ill to agree to go into hospital when they need to. The sections likely to affect most schizophrenia sufferers are *Section 4*, lasting up to 72 hours for emergencies, *Section 2*, lasting up to 28 days, for assessment and treatment, and *Section 3*, lasting up to 6 months, for treatment.

Patients may be admitted to hospital under these sections in the interests of their health *or* their safety *or* for the protection of other persons. It is important to note that they may be admitted *in the interests of their health* as many professionals believe they should only be admitted in the interests of their safety or for the protection of other persons. This can be disastrous for sufferers as neither of the latter two grounds might apply while the individual becomes irreversibly damaged waiting for urgently needed treatment. Families may wish to refer to the up-to-date version of the *THE CODE OF PRACTICE, Mental Health Act 1983*, available from the HMSO, London, which now highlights this particular ground for admission.

An approved social worker (ASW) will normally make the application for the sufferer's admission to hospital under section, but the *nearest relative* may also do this, (given, of course, that doctors are recommending this admission). If an ASW is unavailable or refuses to make the application after assessing the sufferer, then a doctor or social worker should explain to the family the rights of the nearest relative in this connection and guide him or her through the procedure. NB: IT IS THE FAMILY'S RIGHT TO HAVE THIS INFOR-MATION AND GUIDANCE. If the information is not forthcoming, then ask for it. The nearest relative is determined by the following list, assuming a minimum age of 18 years, in order of priority:

- husband or wife
- son or daughter
- father or mother
- brother or sister
- grandparent
- grandchild
- uncle or aunt
- nephew or niece

Where two relatives have equal priority, then the elder of the two will be the choice, and half-blood relationships will take second place. Where the patient normally resides with a relative, then that one will be the nearest relative. If the patient has lived with a non-relative as husband or wife for at least six months prior to admission to hospital then that person is considered to be the nearest relative (unless one has now deserted the other). If the patient has lived with a non-relative, but not as husband or wife, for five years, then the person is considered to be a relative, but not necessarily the nearest relative.

These rules may seem complicated but they are worth noting as the *nearest relative* has special rights under the current mental health legislation. The right to make application for the sufferer's admission to hospital has frequently brought to an end potentially tragic delays which can hold this up for days, weeks or months.

Families have no say in the patient's treatment but they do have rights if they wish their relative to be discharged. These rights will be explained to them at the time of the admission, when patients will also be advised of their right to appeal to a Review Tribunal. This often causes families further distress, worrying lest their relative should be taken off the section at the Tribunal, which in effect can free patients from the requirement to accept treatment before they have had an opportunity to gain insight into their need for this. It is therefore important that the nearest relative, or an appointee, should make arrangements to represent the family's concern to the Tribunal panel.

### (9) State Benefits

This system can seem like a veritable jungle to the uninitiated, but the first and most important thing to remember is to submit *sick certificates* to your local Department of Social Security (DSS) from the start of your relative's illness. In case, as so often happens, this is not recognized for some time, make a note of the first time that help was sought from your GP and from anyone else and remind the doctor of this when an illness has been acknowledged, asking for an appropriately back-dated certificate which you can submit to the DSS. It may be helpful to note the following benefits:

### Statutory Sick Pay

This is for those who are working when they become ill. Since 1986, employers have been responsible for paying this for the first twenty-eight weeks of an employee's sick leave.

### Invalidity Benefit (IB)

Invalidity benefit is not means tested and therefore unaffected by any change in the financial circumstances of the claimant. It is payable at the end of the first twenty-eight weeks of sick leave if the claimant has enough 'paid-up' stamps for the relevant twelve-month working period. Individuals on this benefit can take advantage of the 'therapeutic earnings' rule which allows them to earn extra money (up to about half of the value of IB) for a limited time in a part-time job which has to be recommended by a doctor and approved by the DSS.

## Severe Disablement Allowance (SDA)

In most cases the claimant has to prove an eighty per cent disability before this is payable. This can be achieved when a chronic sufferer is clearly going to be permanently unfit for any kind of work. It is unlikely to apply to most sufferers who may be well enough to work intermittently. However, anyone who has been incapable of work for six months and who is between sixteen and twenty years of age can qualify, as can older individuals who can prove they have been too ill to work since before their twentieth birthday. The benefit can be topped up by Income Support and is also subject to the 'therapeutic earnings' rule.

## Disability Living Allowance (DLA)

This has replaced the old Attendance Allowance and Mobility Allowance and there are various bands of payment with both a 'care' element and a 'mobility' element. The rules are complicated but many schizophrenia sufferers should qualify for the lower or middle bands under the 'care' element for the following sorts of reasons:

(1) not being able to organize and prepare a main meal for themselves.

(2) needing to be reminded and monitored by others when it comes to taking their prescribed medication.

(3) needing to have someone 'keep an eye' on them each day.

There are various other factors that might be relevant to any one individual. Those who are awarded a middle band payment and who live independently may qualify for an extra benefit Supplementary Disability Pension (SDP), so check this out.

Do anyway consider applying for DLA for your relative if he or she has been ill for three months and looks like remaining so for at least as long again.

## Income Support

This is the mainstay now of many sufferers' income; it is a means tested benefit so will be reduced or not payable if the claimant has a certain amount of capital; check on up-to-date rules on this. Sufferers who draw Income Support and who are unable to work because of their illness should regularly submit medical certificates to the DSS and after six months they will be entitled to a disability premium which should boost their benefit by nearly half as much again and allow an earnings disregard of £15 per week.

Income Support can be claimed as a top-up to other benefits such as SDA and brings with it a package of other privileges such as help with NHS prescriptions, dental treatment, spectacles and fares for hospital treatment. It also entitles claimants to maximum housing benefit which amounts to a hundred per cent of their rent and eighty per cent of their Council Tax.

## Social Fund

This replaced the old Single Payments system which used to cover claims for replacement of essential items and for emergencies. It comprises two schemes; (1) *Community Care Grants* which are intended for helping disabled people to lead independent lives in the community and are claimable by sufferers leaving hospital, or some other institution, to help them settle down independently in the community, and (2) *Budgeting Loans* which are interest-free loans to cover certain items of furniture and domestic expenses. Repayments will be deducted from existing benefits so the DSS will first check that the individual can afford these.

## Typical Problems

Claiming benefits involves much filling in of forms and 'getting into the system' can prove laborious and frustrating. The same problems tend to crop up again each time claimants change their 'status' as, for example, when they are discharged from hospital or change their accommodation.

If your relative is too unwell to claim and draw benefits, or refuses to do so, then ask for advice at your local DSS as a carer can become an appointee for the claimant.

## (10) Voluntary Sector

There are several voluntary organizations which are particularly concerned with schizophrenia. These include the National Schizophrenia Fellowship (NSF), SANE (Schizophrenia: A National Emergency), and the Schizophrenia Association of Great Britain (SAGB). The first two also concern themselves with other types of mental illness and SANE runs a telephone help-line which is open during evenings and weekends. There are 160 local NSF self-help groups throughout England, Wales and Northern Ireland and the fellowship puts on conferences which are suitable for sufferers and carers and service providers alike. It also publishes and recommends literature on schizophrenia, as does SANE. The SAGB and SANE are very much concerned with research and all three organizations send out Newsletters to their members.

## Summing Up

Ideally, this type of 'user-friendly' guide will include 'Further Reading' lists (the voluntary organizations should be able to help here) and 'Useful Addresses' Lists (which should include local sources of guidance and help).

## CHAPTER 9

# Dealing with Specific Problems

We have already noted the sort of help that will be required if we are to meet the needs which sufferers and carers have highlighted in Chapters 6 and 7. Not surprisingly, most of these have been concerned with damage limitation; they have been concerned with protecting individuals who have the acute form of the illness from slipping into the disabling Type II syndrome. But what about all those who have already suffered that fate?

## The Chronic Form of Schizophrenia

The vast majority of Type II syndrome sufferers now live in the community and they and their carers have some very special needs which are rarely met at present. It is in these cases that support has to be ongoing if it is to be effective. The negative symptoms of schizophrenia preclude much likelihood of their victims taking the initiative to ensure they obtain the help they need. Furthermore, these symptoms also make it unlikely that they will persevere with any services they are offered unless they are constantly encouraged to do so. Because of this, the more severely handicapped represent a potentially forgotten population and unless they have family support or live in hostel accommodation there is a real risk that they will 'slip through the net'.

If chronically ill sufferers are in danger of being forgotten, then this is a fate they share with any carers trying to support them. These in turn are more often than not just left to get on with it and, as we noted earlier, they are often women, sometimes elderly mothers, providing twenty-four hours a day care and struggling to cope in an unappreciative world. Two social workers have described what this can be like:

> 'I'm shouting for help and they pass by, social workers, doctors, nurses.
> I can't make them hear what it's like for me or get them to unlock the

door with their knowledge and understanding – I want to help him but I need to know how.'[1]

What can we do to help? First of all, anything we can do to involve chronically ill sufferers outside of the home has to be a positive move. Those who live alone will deteriorate further if they lie on their beds all day or sit staring into space for hours on end. Those who live with carers will not thrive if they are at home with them twenty-four hours a day and nor will their carers. Both need some space and sufferers with negative symptoms need stimulation if they are to enjoy any quality of life. How can we provide this?

## A Routine

In its own small way, a bus or car journey to another building can provide some stimulation for individuals otherwise trapped in their homes all day. It does not matter too much if they do just sit down on arrival in much the same way as they were doing before they left home. What does matter is that they are being involved in a routine which demands a certain amount of effort to get ready and make the journey. Also, when they arrive, they are at least amongst a different group of people. Equally important, carers can then indulge in the normal everyday event in our society of waving family members off to work, or wherever, and getting on with their own lives for a few precious hours. This is something that many carers have no chance to do.

## Stimulation

Further stimulation can be attempted once the sufferer has become used to a routine of getting out regularly. This can often be achieved if we understand the need to urge and encourage participation constantly in any available activities. The impetus rarely comes from within; it is others who have to make the running and provide the impetus for action of any kind, be it a pencilled drawing, a game of snooker, or joining the group to go on a walk. When we have persuaded such sufferers to take part in this way, it is easy to over-rate our achievement, particularly if the individuals show an aptitude or taste for the activity. It is easy to believe that they will want to have another go the next time the opportunity arises; this is often not the case. Next time, we soon discover that we have to start anew and find a way of motivating them all over again. They can become quite involved each time but often find no motivation to have another go; there is no learning process as such.

However, the temporary stimulation is so much more positive than just watching the deterioration that takes place when this is missing. The quality of life can be seen to improve during these short bouts of activity, however modest.

Some individuals do gradually become more involved in what is going on around them, if we are proactive and persevere on an ongoing basis. During the years I have run the Needs Based groups discussed in Chapter 12, I have on several occasions invited sufferers with quite severe 'negative' symptoms to come along to a session because they have shown a passing interest in doing so, and I have been delighted to find them attending regularly, playing a passive but valued role in the group.

Similarly, chronic sufferers can become exceptionally loyal and regular attenders at clubs and other resources provided for them *once they have become used to them* and found a niche for themselves. Up until that point, it is essential that someone makes sure they get there each time. That is where we come in. Chronically ill sufferers will not take advantage of resources just because we provide them; they will only do this initially if we make it easy and painless for them to attend. By 'initially', we might be talking about the first half-a-dozen times and then the odd times later when they tire of making the effort. Ideally, there will be provision for transport, but if this is not the case then we need to find some other way of achieving this. 'Fetching and carrying' for a while can be more rewarding and productive than occasionally visiting an inactive sufferer in an isolated bedsitter or one who is homebound and whose carer's frustration serves as an indictment of our work.

## Respite

There will always be some chronic sufferers who will not come out of the home. They and others like them used to spend their lives in the old mental hospitals. Although such individuals were singled out as the victims of *institutionalization*, there were more opportunities for stimulation in these large communities than in an isolated bedsit or the bedroom of a family home. We should not leave these individuals to live on their own with little or no contact with other human beings, nor should we condemn carers to struggle on under similar circumstances. Until such time as alternatives can be offered for all of them, we must not desert the severe casualties of this potentially cruel illness.

We should visit these sufferers regularly, whether they live alone or with carers, and we should try to meet the need of the latter for some respite care, preferably in the form of holidays, and also for a few hours break each week.

One way this ongoing help can be provided would be to set up the sort of befriending service which is now becoming popular, with lay volunteers giving up some of their spare time, with training and back-up support from professionals and other workers.

## Summing Up

A lot can be achieved for chronic sufferers and for their carers if we take the approach 'What can we do to help you?' and apply ourselves to adapting our practice to their needs rather than providing resources which they are unable to use. Our achievements in this direction may seem to us to be modest at best, but they can make a dramatic difference to the quality of life for this forgotten population. We really must keep trying.

## Marriage in Schizophrenia

First of all, it is worth noting that although marriages are fewer and more at risk in this illness than those in the general population, many sufferers are happily married. What is usually needed from 'the system' is awareness that there are specific times of risk when an offer of help may be appreciated and also specific circumstances that may demand nothing more than a little time and moral support.

## A Time of Risk

One such time can, for some couples where the wife is the sufferer, be the starting of a family. Nowadays, the mother-to-be will be advised to discontinue her medication during at least part of the pregnancy and it may be that this will be good for her baby but not for her. Thus the expectant mother can be exposed to risk during pregnancy and she can be similarly exposed to risk of relapse following the birth; a time of hormonal upheaval. She will also be burdened with new responsibilities and with the continual demands of a new baby. All in all, there is every reason to offer these mothers extra time and support during the child's first year to help them avoid the risk of breakdown and to check whether or not the family may need some ongoing help, probably of a practical kind.

One such example occurred with a young mother after the birth of her third child. Still very vulnerable, she was becoming more and more exhausted trying to cope and was having trouble getting up in the mornings after her husband had gone to work two hours earlier. We were able to enlist a Home Help for one hour each weekday morning (on the grounds of avoiding further breakdown in the mother) to make sure she got up in time in the mornings and to help her organize the two older children. The Home Help would then take them to school, while the mother fed the new baby. After eight months, this young woman was able to cope on her own. If handled tactfully and respectfully, this sort of back-up can help a new mother through a potentially exhausting phase of her life.

### Particularly Trying Circumstances

A rather different problem can occur where the sufferer becomes too damaged to fulfil the role of 'soul-mate' and confidante for the partner, making the latter feel very much alone. This seems to be most difficult if the couple have a young family and if the damaged partner is the man. If the woman then has to take most of the responsibility for running the family and home and also has to cushion her husband from the outside world, then this can be a reversal of what she would expect from her marriage. Even today, society still expects the male to be the wage-earner and the backbone of the marriage. When this may not be possible and most of the leaning has to be the other way round, then this dilemma can threaten the balance of the marriage.

In some cases, we can help to fill the gap that has been left for the damaged sufferer's spouse and offer a listening ear and our moral support. This sort of support can often provide what is needed to enable the individual to build on the positive aspects of the marriage, thus benefiting both partners. Again, the need for this support is likely to be spasmodic and, ideally, it can be provided when the client seeks it. As such, it is an economical use of resources when compared with the potential burden of the breakdown of the family. I have known families thrive remarkably well with such occasional support because the healthy partner has found the strength to 'soldier on' at the most difficult times.

### Dealing With Typical Everyday Problems

If there is not to be constant friction and frustration over problems resulting from this illness, then we need to help carers and sufferers find ways of resolving them. If we are not careful, families become submerged in a culture summed up by 'Oh, but you see it's his illness' and this is not helpful for anyone. One of the reasons that we, the service providers, need to understand and appreciate the symptoms of schizophrenia is so that we can find ways of helping sufferers and carers cope positively with the problems these raise, rather than to succumb to them. Let's take a look at a typical example of such a problem.

## (1) 'He Won't Get Out of Bed in the Morning!'

This common problem comes up again and again. Sometimes I hear responses like 'Well, does that really matter?'. Clearly, the answer to that is 'Yes, it does'. First, a mother is concerned enough about it to be mentioning it to us and seeking our advice. Second, it can be injurious to the individual's health and progress to lie in bed for hours. How can we help to resolve this 'evergreen' problem?

First of all, what does the mother mean? Does the sufferer just get up late in the morning or, rather differently, does he or she lie in bed most of the day? Depending on the reply, we should be looking at one or two different issues, i.e.:

### (i) NOT GETTING UP FIRST THING IN THE MORNING

If it is just that Jim won't get up first thing in the morning, we need to ascertain why this upsets the mother. Sometimes we will find that she believes he could be employed if it were not for this lying in bed when others are rushing off to work. This if often a case of 'putting the cart before the horse' and, if so, we can explain that Jim is not yet ready for work and discuss this a little further − in other words, having a 'normal' lifestyle does not make someone well; this comes from being well. If problems still remain over Jim getting up late, then we can look at each of these in turn and discuss any other factors which may be appropriate such as a need to sleep later in the morning if one cannot sleep at night or a need for 'something to get up early for'. This sort of discussion can lead to acceptable compromise − if the mother no longer believes that staying in bed for half the morning is in itself hindering her son's recovery, then the problem may resolve itself. If, on the other hand, carer and sufferer both believe the time has come for change, then it should be possible to find 'something to get up early for' on at least some mornings each week, thus providing the needed incentive and opportunity for developing a more normal routine.

### (ii) LYING IN BED ALL MORNING OR MOST OF THE DAY

If Jim is spending hours and hours in bed during the daytime, then this is a different matter. It is understandable that the mother feels frustrated about this and it is certainly not helpful for sufferers to adopt this lifestyle. It can serve to reinforce any tendency to turn night-time into day and this continuing inactivity breeds inactivity and lethargy. Where this is happening, a compromise is needed which allows for more stimulation and intermittent, rather than continuous, resting.

One way of tackling this is to find an incentive for being up by noon at the latest. For a start, the mother could be advised to make sure that refreshments are only available 'downstairs' and that lunch is prepared at midday and cleared away a reasonable time after this. Later, it might be possible to help her further by arranging for some activity or day care facility to be offered Jim at 2pm on, say, two days a week. This would probably necessitate a lift being arranged in the first instance, but such an arrangement can provide the initial steps to developing a proper daily routine. In Chapter 11, Sally and Stephen describe their own experiences in achieving this.

### (2) Alec Plays His Music all Night

This is another 'evergreen' problem caused, of course, by the 'turning the night into day' syndrome that is so common in this illness. Sufferers affected this way find it hard to understand that when they 'come to life' late at night and at last throw off some of the lethargy of the daytime, this is no cause for rejoicing by the rest of the household! If there is one thing more frustrating than having a family member staying in bed all day, it is being kept awake by the same individual most of the night. This understandably brings accusations such as 'he's only up all night because he sleeps all day' and these can only be dealt with by careful explanation about the upturning of the 24-hour body clock that can be part of a schizophrenic illness.

However, although it is important that those most affected should understand that this is one more problem which is not the fault of the sufferer, such understanding will not make up for losing a night's sleep. The environment promoted by this sort of deprivation and frustration will do nothing at all to serve the sufferer's interests now or in the long term. If Alec does not seem to be receptive to everyone's concerns on this, then it may be a good idea to draw up some HOUSE RULES and these are discussed at the end of this section.

### (3) Mavis Won't Take Her Medication Properly

This is another 'evergreen' problem, for reasons we have already discussed earlier in the book. Here again we need a little more information, in other words, (a) is she behaving this way because she has unpleasant side effects with the medication? or (b) is she blaming lingering symptoms of her illness, such as feelings of lethargy, on her medication? or (c) does she believe she is not ill and therefore has no reason to take medication?

If we sit down and talk with Mavis and her mother, we should soon be able to assess which of these sorts of reasons applies in this case. If it turns out to be (a) and Mavis is having unpleasant side effects, then we can arrange for the supervising doctor to be made aware of this.

If the 'side effects' turn out to be probable symptoms of the illness, as in (b), then we can discuss this carefully with mother and daughter, explaining that it is often only when sufferers are becoming really well on medication that they begin to appreciate they are losing symptoms they originally believed to be 'side effects'. We can recommend back-up reading material to them or suggest that Mavis might like to meet with recovered sufferers or join the type of group discussed in Chapter 12, so that she can compare her own experiences with other sufferers. It is important that we should be prepared to repeat the whole exercise several times, to go over the same points and to answer fully any remaining questions. This sort of approach can often lead to an improvement; where it doesn't, it can still be true that 'a problem shared is a problem halved', particularly if we have taken the time to clarify what is really causing the concern and have dealt with any previous negative feelings.

If (c) applies and Mavis does not intend to take her medication, then it may be too late to do anything about this, beyond seeking the help of the supervising doctor and making sure that the mother has enough backing to persuade her daughter to persevere with the medication the next time around. As we have noted, this sort of problem resolves itself only when sufferers themselves recognize the necessity to take their medication.

## House Rules

These imply recognition of the fact that, although schizophrenia will inevitably raise problems for those having to live with the illness, it is essential to find a way for the needs of everyone concerned to be protected as far as possible. If a compromise can be achieved, then this will minimize frustration which can lead to argument and unconstructive criticism. The latter helps no-one, least of all the sufferer.

HOUSE RULES should include only matters of major importance, if they are to avoid becoming meaningless. If any of the three everyday problems we have discussed above remained unresolved they would (and frequently have) become matters of grave concern to the rest of the household. Other families have drawn up the following types of rules to deal with them, taking account of both the sufferer's and the rest of the family's viewpoint:

(1) Jim must get up by noon each day or miss meals until the evening-time. He agrees to go out for some pre-arranged activity on two afternoons each week.

In return, Jim must not be bothered by other members of the household before noon each day and there will be no comments about his staying in bed until that time.

(2) Everyone in the household recognizes that Alec is unable to sleep during the night and no-one will comment on this.

In return, Alec must not make the sort of noise during the night that will keep the rest of the household awake; i.e., if he wants to play music he will use ear-phones to do this.

(3) If Mavis wants to continue to live with her mother, then she must take her prescribed medication.

The third example is not a compromise; it may typically represent the last stand of a lone parent at the end of her tether when the sufferer never gains insight into her need for medication and is impossibly difficult to live with because of this. It sometimes works...!

## Violence in This Illness

Violence is the one aspect of schizophrenia that is well publicized; in fact, it is the *only* aspect of the illness that is familiar to everyone. This is sad; violence is so uncommon a feature of schizophrenia as to be the exception rather than the rule. When it occurs it is likely to be the result of untreated or neglected symptoms leading to the sort of terror that could justify a 'self-defence' verdict in a seemingly unprovoked attack. Alternatively, serious violence features in a tiny minority of sufferers whose psychopathic personalities make a diagnosis of schizophrenia an incidental of little consequence. Meanwhile, this perpetuated image of violence in schizophrenia, originally kindled by the media, causes the majority of sufferers profound pain.

That said, there is no doubt that a few families live in fear of attack from an ill schizophrenic relative. All those working with this illness have a responsibility to watch out for warning signs of breakdown or relapse. In particular, we should be listening to any fears expressed by carers and also be sensitive to any signs of nervousness or tension in them. This is very important as sometimes there is collusion with a potentially aggressive sufferer, in some cases through loyalty and in others through fear. This should not be allowed to happen.

In those few cases where it seems that a sufferer's paranoid symptoms cannot be relieved, either because these are not responsive to the available drug treatment or through lack of co-operation and compliance, then unpredictable and violent behaviour can put others at risk.

Sometimes the individual's freedom may have to be curtailed, but this will usually be a short-term measure so it may also be necessary for close relatives to put their homes 'out of bounds' to the sufferer. Fortunately, such cases are not common but this does not make them any less difficult for families who do find themselves in this situation. It is not acceptable that we turn the other way as sometimes happens when a lone mother, for instance, lives in terror of the dreaded knock at the door. She has the right to be protected and may need to be encouraged to take out an injunction, or to take whatever other action is required, and she must be supported in this. Perhaps we can imagine just how painful taking such steps might be for a mother who knows that it is an illness that has made her son or daughter into a violent stranger?

## A Lesser Problem

Much easier to cope with, if we provide appropriate advice and support, is the situation where a household is 'tyrannized' by unreasonable demands from an unwell sufferer. This may happen if relatives feel they should humour the sufferer because he or she is ill or because they fear the individual will become aggressive if they do not comply. So long as we note what is happening, this is a situation where we can intervene positively because the behaviour does not stem from the terror of unrelieved symptoms. It is behaviour which has been learned and which has been unwittingly encouraged. As such it can be 'unlearned' and has to be, because it should not be tolerated; this is the sort of situation that can lead to family breakdown. The whole household will need moral support for a while and guidance on setting up some appropriate house rules as discussed above.

## Comment

These then are some of the specific everyday problems which may lead to family breakdown if we don't intervene and find ways of helping to solve them. They provoke the sort of fears and frustrations which grind away, gradually undermining the carer's resolve to 'soldier on'.

They are very different from the other major cause of sufferers losing family support. This is when the carers experience just one too many trauma. Far from our foreseeing and helping to prevent such a tragedy, it may be quite the reverse. Families in this situation often finally give up because of the way professionals treat them at such times. Consider; two carers in this book have referred to the professionals involved in their family crisis as 'the enemy'. Can we imagine how this must feel?

## The Trauma of Crisis Situations

I have known too many relatives who have been at the point of 'disappearing off the face of the earth' by the time health professionals have at last accepted their responsibility to acknowledge a sufferer's breakdown. A few have in fact fled because this did not happen. They have left everything that mattered to them, setting up home elsewhere. Can we imagine the feelings of guilt, deprivation and despair they have to live with for the rest of their lives? Consider the fate now of the relative they tried so hard to support...

If we are to protect sufferers from losing those they need, then we have to recognize the plight of families struggling to cope with this illness. We have to realize that to ignore their pleas for help when their relative is relapsing yet again, is to ignore their continuing experience of life with this illness. We have to challenge our own assumptions, including the sort that imply they 'are fussing too much' or 'trying to get rid of their relative'. If so, why on earth are they involved? Why are they still here and suffering all the inconveniences of a returning psychosis if they want to get rid of the sufferer?

Similarly, we have to overcome an innate resistance to acknowledge this illness in attractive and seemingly able young people. These potentially well 'acute' sufferers are very much at risk because of our innate reluctance to associate them with schizophrenia and because of their ability to confuse all comers. Mary and Bill's daughter ran into similar dangers as John because of this. The latter has not been rescued from his psychotic nightmare eighteen months later...

In short, a needs based approach to dealing with families threatened by crisis is (1) to listen to them and to treat them as partners in care (2) to investigate carefully the causes of their concern (3) to note anomalies between their reports and our observation of the sufferer at the time of assessment (4) to check other sources for an explanation of these differences and (5) to check what has happened in the past when the sufferer has been relapsing. We might do well to bear in mind a comment made by a recent inquiry panel: 'Nothing predicts behaviour like behaviour'[2]; we can learn from the past, as families have to.

Far too often, professional intervention at a time of pending crisis amounts to assessing sufferers in an interview situation in which they usually excel and then denying the testimony of families and others closely involved. The last person we are helping is the individual we seem to be 'protecting'. We have to do better than this because this is a waste of our most precious mental health resource; the human resource.

## CHAPTER 10

# An Effective Resource

In the last chapter we looked at ways in which professionals and other workers can help with specific problems raised by this illness. What other resources can we provide in the community for sufferers and carers? Let's take a look at a 'purpose made' needs based resource that has catered for up to eighty sufferers at any one time during the past four and a half years.

## A Needs Based Resource

St Paul's Centre is a thriving 'drop-in'/day centre based in a small church near the centre of a busy town. Since its opening in July 1989 this has represented a partnership between the NHS, the Anglican church and a local National Schizophrenia Fellowship group. In the new 'contract culture' climate, this is about to change and the future is unclear at the time of writing. However, those of us who have had the privilege of setting up this resource and running it have so far been given a free hand 'to get on with it' and to determine its philosophy and policy. This in turn has provided a rare opportunity to 'try and test' a model from which others can benefit as well as our own clients.

## The Background

This project originated from an offer during 1985 from a regional health authority to local voluntary groups to make bids for funding to improve their own services for the mentally ill. The local NSF group asked its members what they felt was most needed and they unanimously backed a sufferer's plea for 'somewhere that belongs to us; where we can go a couple of evenings a week and know we've got a right to be there!'

From this modest beginning, the venture mushroomed and by some strange fluke the group found itself taking on a little church, still used by its small congregation on Sundays. Along the way, the local health authority took over ultimate responsibility for the resource and for employing and paying its manager. This manager-to-be was a mental health professional who also represented the local NSF group; myself.

After several false starts due to the *Not in my Back Yard* syndrome, we eventually gave up waiting for our 'real home' and opened up in a derelict old hospital building round the corner from the church in July 1989. We finally moved into the church in January 1991. By then, we had around fifty clients (*members*), a paid manager, seven voluntary workers and the back-up support of a community psychiatric nurse.

Now we open on five days a week, have sixty-five members on our books (contributing to over 5,000 attendances a year), a paid manager, two extra voluntary workers, the same amount of CPN support and five hours input from occupational therapy technicians. The co-ordinator of the NSF group – Ena – has acted as unpaid deputy manager from the day we opened.

As may be clear, this very large resource has run on a shoestring since it opened and we consequently spend most of our own spare time begging for funding for extra members of staff. Meanwhile, the commitment of our voluntary workers has been impressive; four have been with us since the centre opened in 1989 and two more joined the team three years ago. Absences for anything other than holidays are almost unheard of. It may be significant that this sort of dedication comes from a staff team made up mostly of carers and sufferers. I have never before had the privilege of working with such a happy and united team.

## Our Members

Nearly all of these have had a schizophrenic illness. We cater for some very capable individuals who are potentially well most of the time, through to some who have for a long time had little contact with the rest of the human race; walking the streets during the day and returning to isolated bedsits or 'bed and breakfast' at night. Around thirty-five per cent of our members are 'acute' sufferers, and about ten per cent of our chronic sufferers have severe negative symptoms. Much to the despair of some of our male population, women represent less than twenty per cent of the membership, emphasizing the more severe long term effects of this illness on male sufferers. Similarly, only three members of ethnic minorities have become members of St Paul's since we opened, reflecting a low representation of these groups in this area[1].

We take young people from the age of seventeen and have no upper age limit; as we have three 'senior citizens' on our staff team we feel it would be inappropriate to turn away clients of a similar age. However, our membership tends to be young, with the largest group being made up of young men in their twenties and thirties.

A few of our members suffer with learning disabilities in addition to their mental illness. Several have minor physical handicaps resulting from 'self-inflicted' damage due to bullying 'voices'. Only one member has a severe physical disability and attends by courtesy of the local Dial-a-Ride service.

Some of our members use other day resources as well as St Paul's; particularly the Industrial Therapy Unit which moved out of the local psychiatric hospital into the community a few years ago. For those who enjoy this sheltered work situation, it is good to hear them refer to this as their 'work' and ourselves as their 'club'. Members tend to come to the centre for periods of at least several years or so; some have been with us since the first few months of its opening. Typically, the frequency of their attendances often decreases as their social life opens up and they become confident enough to take up new opportunities.

## Members' Committee

Around eighteen months ago, several members felt sufficiently involved to set up a committee and this presently consists of six members who have the final say on all extra-curricular events at the centre. Up to now they have initiated several new ventures, such as a 'crib marathon' which raised money for the local homeless population, afternoon quizzes, and several excellent concert evenings. They also liaise with the staff team and this helps us to ensure we keep more closely in touch with the needs of our members. The committee's names and photos are displayed on a board so that new or more reserved members know whom to approach if they want to discuss anything about the centre with their peers rather than with ourselves.

## The Programme

This has evolved in response to the expressed needs of our members. This has meant that one or two activities have been attempted that have not survived. One was a welcomed opportunity for football coaching and practice, but the arrangement broke down after a few months because of transport problems. Some others have been turned down at source because of their impracticality, usually because of the expense involved. A few have been kept 'on hold' for potentially more affluent times in the future. The following list covers the sort of activities and services currently offered:

- Cards and other table games
- Table tennis and snooker
- Carpet Bowls
- Badminton Club
- Piano and modern-type keyboard
- Music centre, radio, tapes and records, and video playback facility
- Round-the-table debate
- Library with books and magazines
- Art and crafts table
- Woodwork
- Silk-screen printing
- Gardening
- 'Ad hoc' counselling
- Needs Based groups
- Information and discussion about mental illness
- Welfare benefits advice
- Advice on other practical matters
- Nursing skills and depot injections.

Tea, coffee and cold drinks are available several times each session and on two days of the week food is served, during the evening social club and on the one full day of the week that the centre is open. We buy all our own food – except for some welcome contributions at Harvest time – and all refreshments are sold at around cost price. These include fresh salads, toasted sandwiches, jacket potatoes through to double-sized mixed grills, with as much emphasis on 'whole foods' as we can get away with. 'French fries' are taboo and this rule represents perhaps the only example of the staff-team ignoring the expressed needs of a few of our clients! Half-a-dozen or so members like to help with the collection of orders, making of tea, delivery of food, and so forth, and the kitchen tends to be the hub of activity that it is in most communities.

Special evenings, such as seasonal parties, concerts, snooker and table-tennis tournaments and, of course, barbeques, include the provision of free banquets prepared by Ena and her kitchen team; supposedly from small profits gleaned from the day-to-day sale of refreshments but owing rather more to her personal generosity and dedication. Ena's approach to improving the quality of life of those trying to cope with this illness has been an example to us all. Having no health professional training, she nevertheless brings countless practical and creative talents to the centre and mothers everyone, including the staff-team. She has taught us all that a combination of *love, respect* and *unruffled calm* works miracles with mental illness. Add to these qualities large helpings of sound *common sense* and we at St Paul's are blessed with a model deputy manager.

### A Success

Our attendance figures and public accolades from local consumer groups and mental health bodies pay tribute to the success of this venture, a venture aimed exclusively at a client population not renowned for taking up or persevering with available resources. Our only regret is that we have had to 'close our books' for the past twelve months owing to continuing lack of funds.

Why, then, has the centre been so successful?

### Our Ethos

Predictably, the ethos at St Paul's is based on the sort of recommendations made throughout this book. It is a Needs Based resource. As we have seen, it came about in response to a suggestion from a sufferer, its policy was planned by a carers' group and its day-to-day programme has evolved from the expressed needs of a continuing stream of sufferers. Our ethos is a user-responsive one and it relies on several main threads:

### (1) Preventive Intervention

This is the mainstay of the ethos of St Paul's; we see no point in watching our clients strive for good health, only to fall by the wayside for the want of a helping hand along the way. We have demonstrated to the satisfaction of those professionals involved with us that our preventive approach has helped to stem the destructive process of the 'revolving door' syndrome. Some of our more vulnerable clients trust us enough now actually to seek help when they feel unwell. Others would not go that far but nevertheless accept our suggestion that we should seek help together; sooner rather than later. This done, some doctors tend not to listen to us or to their nurse colleagues but others do and it can be very rewarding to see members come through a 'sticky patch' unharmed because of early intervention. This encourages them to trust their own insight and ourselves next time around.

## (2) Terms of Reference For Members

(i) Our referral system allows for all comers to come and meet with us and to settle down at the centre or to self-select themselves out, thus avoiding unnecessary rejection. After a dozen or so visits, newcomers automatically become members.

(ii) Members come and go as they please. Although some of them let us know when they're leaving each time or telephone to say they 'won't be in today' with a touching old-fashioned courtesy, all are free to come as often or as little as they like. Many isolated sufferers settle down at St Paul's after months of popping in for ten minutes or so several times a week. Its so rewarding to one day find them waiting outside for the doors to be opened.

This would not happen if they were originally allocated certain times and days. We resist all attempts by professionals to allocate their clients to named days at St Paul's in order that they comply with a prepared timetable. We have found that one way to spark off incentive in our members and to reactivate their motivation is to leave it to them to decide if and when they come. It is their choice and when they make this themselves their self-respect soars in a way it cannot do if they attend because someone else has arranged for them to do so. Furthermore, because *they* make the decision it becomes a very worthwhile one for them.

Nevertheless, we seek help from involved professionals if a prospective member is a chronic sufferer who might need help with getting to the centre and settling into a routine as we discussed in the last chapter.

(iii) We make it clear to prospective members that they will come to St Paul's for as long as they like. I have seen much effort and work with sufferers invalidated because they have been given a limited time at a resource. Why should they make a serious commitment in these circumstances, setting themselves up for a crashing let-down? Everyone who comes to St Paul's knows that they have joined a 'club' and can continue to be a member for as long as they want to. This recognizes that there is no cure for this type of mental illness so there is a need for ongoing resources rather than temporary measures.

(iv) Finally, we have had to draw up some basic 'house rules' and these revolve around the comforts and needs of the whole community.

For example, we cannot tolerate drug abuse and drug pushing, borrowing (and not returning) money, and inexcusably threatening behaviour. Five members have been banned (after adequate warning) since we first opened; three have asked to become members again and one of these has so far been welcomed back, initially on a trial basis.

## (3) Social Interaction

We recognize the main difficulty which many sufferers have with socializing; their impaired ability to initiate conversation or to join in what is going on around them. If we leave several members in the early stages of their joining us to socialize, we can guarantee to find them sitting quietly together staring into space. At all times we make sure that staff are involved informally with our members, initiating social interaction and much needed stimulation. We expect this to be a continuing process where our more handicapped sufferers are concerned, but it has been a joy to note a gradual growth of confidence in more able members and their increasing tendency to involve less skilled individuals in conversation and activities in the centre. Similarly, it has been a bonus to watch members make relationships which extend beyond the centre and help to enrich their lives in the larger community outside St Paul's.

## (4) Families and Other Carers

Our members willingly share their resource with families and other carers, who come and go as they please. They are particularly welcoming to voluntary workers who are carers, finding it rewarding to talk to 'someone else's Mum'.

Often we are in touch with members' families through our work in the NSF group or because they have been introduced to us by colleagues. Sometimes, however, all attempts to reach them have been unsuccessful. One of the most rewarding parts of our work is when a young member asks in a studiedly casual manner if it would be OK to bring his Mum or Dad in to meet us? Nevertheless, we would rather meet relatives right from the start. This enables us to liaise with them and sometimes avert a threatened crisis because of this.

## Summing Up

The ethos of St Paul's encompasses a medical model in that:

(1) We seek to educate members about their illness and the role of their medication.

(2) We seek medical intervention when we see they are vulnerable.

(3) We encourage nurses to monitor our members and to give depot injections at the centre, so that the latter can take advantage of this service during a social visit without any inconvenience or the sort of embarrassment that some sufferers associate with attending a formal depot injection clinic.

However, our ethos clearly represents a social model too, in that:

(1) We reject the formalities commonly found in other large mental health resources.

(2) We are very much concerned with helping members to maximize their quality of life.

(3) We emphasize opportunities for mixing socially and for practising social skills.

(4) We encourage members to set themselves realistic goals and gradually realize their full potential.

(5) We offer guidance on everyday practical matters.

(6) We strive to provide an environment in which everyone feels they 'belong' and we encourage members to treat St Paul's as a club, in the way that best suits each individual.

This psycho-social approach reflects, as far as we can presently achieve this, the methods of working recommended throughout this book. These are based on the premise that schizophrenia sufferers, like the rest of us, can only take advantage of social opportunities if they can keep well enough to do this. We have to meet both of these needs if they are to attain an acceptable quality of life. A health professional told the staff-team that when someone mentioned St Paul's recently, one of her colleagues said 'I always associate the centre with laughter not with illness'. This reference to the fact that St Paul's is more often than not resounding with laughter reminded us that most sufferers will eventually find their own way through, given half a chance to do so. Schizophrenia does not have to be bad news and we hope our members will continue to be wonderful ambassadors for others struggling with this illness.

## A Few Considerations

I hope that this description of our model of a day care resource may be useful for others looking for ways to meet the needs of this client group. Let's now take a closer look at several aspects of our experience which might be usefully taken into account before anyone embarks on a similar enterprise.

## A Resource Which Just Grew and Grew!

Up until now, the running costs of St Paul's have been very low indeed but this, of course, has been due to much good will from a dedicated band of supporters. In the new 'contract culture', this is probably not to be recommended; the basics should be costed and allowed for, with the voluntary effort providing the trimmings of the service.

Indeed, I am not sure we would have been prepared to take the chances we have taken over the past four to five years if we were just starting out again now. It was originally supposed that we would provide for around twenty members; in the event, we were encouraged to continue to take all-comers and we had a potential membership of ninety at one point. In a way, the life of St Paul's has reflected the lives of many sufferers; we have soldiered on in a system providing little more than 'first-aid' treatment with each new crisis.

This has had its positive side, of course, in that we were clearly free to get on and do the best we could. There were times when staff holidays became something of a luxury for those taking them and a potential crisis for the rest of the team. This sort of predicament led to our very much appreciating our members' support and co-operation at these times and resulted in our consulting them at every stage in our development. This sort of mutually dependent situation always helps to discourage the dreaded 'them and us' culture which can undermine so much of the work carried out in the mental health field. Given that we never forget these invaluable lessons and continue to regard St Paul's as a resource which owes its success to its members, its staff-team and its supporters, then I feel it can only gain in the future by the provision of reasonable staffing levels and more adequate funding.

## Back-up From NHS Staff

(1)  We have enjoyed back-up support since the start of this project from a community psychiatric nursing team which specializes in long-term care; for the past two years this has been provided by a rota with each of the CPNs taking it in turns to work a session at

the centre. This has proved to be a mutually benefical arrangment and it is hoped that CPNs will always be involved with St. Paul's.

(2) Similarly, the input by the Occupational Therapy department has proved valuable and well appreciated.

(3) For a brief ten-month period an enlightened psychiatrist – an old colleague of ours – demonstrated that medical input at St Paul's could be rewarding and productive. Responsible for the treatment of a third of our members, he provided a once-weekly clinic and also kept in touch with us to check if we had any concerns; if so, he would call in and deal with these when passing. Similarly, he was happy for his patients to approach him themselves whenever he was at the centre; a courtesy which was appreciated, but never abused. This was, of course, a practical example of Needs Based psychiatry in the community; his patients reported happily, 'he really listens!' and we in turn were able to intervene on their behalf at the first signs of threatened relapse.

Following this doctor's retirement, we found the medical input proved less rewarding. The centre was in effect used as an venue for a formal once-weekly clinic – for roughly the same proportion of our members as before – with no consultation or contact with most of the staff closely involved with these individuals. From our point of view this was a denial of the potential benefits to be gained from proper communication with us and ignored the fact that our clients often sought this liaison themselves as a natural way to serve their own welfare and interests! We eventually gave up on this; it seemed to us then – and indeed has done so throughout most of our time at St Paul's – that we have shared the situation reported by so many families, having no proper mechanism by which to share our day-to-day experience of our members with those supervising their treatment. Meanwhile, CPNs have only sometimes been able to pass on to them any concerns we might have at the appropriate and critical time.

We feel this 'hit and miss' system has served our members short and we hope that in time our first ten-month experience of medical input at St Paul's will be seen as a 'damage limitation' model that can be used to provide effective support for this and other day resources.

## Extra Staffing

When it comes to permanent (paid) staff, to complement the manager and deputy manager, we shall be looking for the sort of qualities we have come to value so much in many of our voluntary workers:

(1) innate common sense

(2) an ability to merge into the crowd and 'lead from the back'

(3) an ability to identify with another's situation

(4) an empathic and approachable manner

(5) a respect for the wishes and opinions of others

(6) an unfailing sense of humour!

A tall order, perhaps, but one we know to be not entirely unrealistic.

## Future Developments

When it comes to moving forward, we have two areas of concern at St Paul's which we are waiting to tackle:

(1) to re-open our books and welcome in those who are asking to come to St Paul's. However, we cannot know at what point saturation will be reached, so we shall have to be careful that we don't once more become the 'victims of our own success'.

(2) to launch a carers' project which we presently have 'on hold'. Although we have always worked with carers along the lines recommended in this book, we have not yet had the opportunity to structure this work. Expected funding for the planned project, together with more appropriate staffing levels, should enable us to go ahead with this during the next eighteen months.

## The Church

Up to now, I have only made passing comment on the involvement of the Church, or more accurately, the local Anglican Diocese, in the advent of this resource. This has been a crucial involvement and one which extended our original modest aims to run a twice-weekly social evening to something beyond our wildest dreams. We understand that the use of a church in this way has created a national precedent which has been the forerunner of a rapidly growing interest in sharing other under-used or disused church buildings with would-be providers of community care.

Originally, this little church served a thriving congregation, which dwindled away when a re-building programme replaced small terraced houses with high-rise blocks of flats. All that remains now is a small, elderly congregation, determined that they shouldn't lose their much loved church. Meanwhile, the building was used very little, other than for its regular Sunday morning services.

When we were approached by Church members interested in finding ways to keep the building in use, they were really suggesting something quite new; the use of an Anglican church for another purpose entirely during the week, whilst preserving its original role and function on Sundays. When they showed the building to our group's committee, this was 'love at first sight'. When I wrote that we believed that the atmosphere in this lovely building could be therapeutic for those trying to cope with a serious mental illness, this caused considerable mirth in the NHS department responsible for preparing it for our use. At the time, there was more concern that some of our prospective members would object to the facility being offered in a church building. This has not proved to be the case, but our members often comment that they find the environment peaceful; my honour is restored!

Five years and two official Church Enquiries later, the proposal came to fruition. Three years after we moved into St Paul's Church, the licence has just been renewed for a further five years.

It is good to report that despite initial fierce opposition from a former headmaster and a small group of parents of children in the primary school next door and from one Church member, we eventually settled comfortably and quietly into the surrounding community. Staff of the school have been friendly and supportive and I have been involved with their activities as a school governor during the past three years. Similarly, our partnership with the Church has proved to be a rewarding one and we can only encourage others wanting to do something like this seriously to consider taking advantage of any similar opportunities.

## CHAPTER 11

# Reality Testing and Other Strategies

We have made several passing references to *reality testing*, a method of working which I pioneered in the early 1980s[1] when working in the community with a young woman who was experiencing destructive lingering symptoms following a first episode of schizophrenia.

We touched on Pat's illness earlier and noted that this manifested itself for her in hearing her parents' voices talking about her father's intention to kill her because she had apparently made her mother fatally ill. Although Pat appeared to make a promising and speedy recovery, it was perhaps not surprising that her paranoid ideas about her father were never far below the surface and she continued to hear both parents' voices still criticizing her whenever she was tired late in the evening; a vulnerable time for many sufferers. It is then that the mind may start to race, with paranoid ideas and false messages returning to confuse and unnerve individuals otherwise doing very well.

If they have had no opportunity to obtain some insight into their illness, then these lingering symptoms will blight hopes that they can leave behind the substance of their psychotic nightmare and resume former trusting relationships. For those who have gained some insight into what has happened to them, as in Pat's case, then sufferers will be better equipped to cope with these lingering symptoms but they will nevertheless be frighteningly real each time they occur. Because of this, it may take a long time before these false messages can be dismissed for what they are. Meanwhile, they undermine the individual's confidence and perpetuate any lingering distrust.

When Pat eventually made an excellent recovery, she maintained that reality testing, as she called it, was one of the most important factors for her in becoming so well. The first stage of this process started quite naturally for her in hospital a month or so following her breakdown, without any involvement by staff. Sometimes she still heard her parents' voices at night-time, as she used to before, and she started to wonder about this because she knew them to be miles away from the hospital. She several times checked this by phoning them and speaking to them at home and as a result she begun to question these voices she was hearing on the ward.

The second stage of Pat's reality testing was initiated a few months after she returned home and confided that she still sometimes heard her parents talking critically about her at night-time, even when she was with them. This second stage lasted around two years and the third stage carried Pat through her first few years away from home.

Her experience made it very clear that this method of working should start from the moment that sufferers are put on medication and should continue right through their recovery until any lingering symptoms have faded away or become manageable. Let's take a look at this three-stage process of reality testing:

## (1) Reassurance in the Aftermath of a Breakdown

As we noted in Chapters 5 and 7, reality testing at this stage is all about seeking and gaining reassurance about the boundary line between reality and the remnants of a psychotic nightmare. This procedure should be continuous throughout the early stages of recovery from a breakdown, enabling the individual to get a grasp of reality and also gradually to gain insight into what has happened. This relies on the sufferer being able to seek this help again and again, as often as needed. It also relies on a 'one-to-one' working relationship with empathic key workers who answer truthfully at all times, avoiding confrontation or collusion with the sufferer's psychotic nightmare, and responding to agitated queries with something like:

> 'Yes, you are quite safe here. Yes, I can understand why you still doubt this, but you really are safe now.'

It is important to remember that we may need to say this five times in an hour if the individual is really agitated, but our patience will be rewarded eventually. Similarly, and as appropriate, we may need to keep confirming something like:

> 'Yes, I know you think you have proof that the doctor is a gunman who has been commissioned to kill you. That must be horribly frightening for you. However, I know him to be a good doctor I have

worked with for years at this hospital and I believe you will soon find this to be true.'

We may need to repeat this over and over again but this becomes less trying if we pause for a moment to consider the implications of this sort of paranoid idea for a terrified sufferer.

Ignoring individuals who are experiencing such ideas is really quite cruel and we risk being guilty of this if we leave sufferers to themselves at this stage of their illness. Attempting to laugh them out of such ideas or to contradict them will also be counterproductive and will be met with hostility and a lack of respect for anything else we might have to say. Remember, delusionary ideas are fixations that are impervious to reason. These ideas represent the truth for individuals who are out of touch with reality. Nevertheless, as the medication starts to undermine the strength of the psychosis, so we can offer comfort and reassurance, while expediting insight by the testing and re-testing of reality.

## (2) Dealing With Lingering and Persistent Symptoms

Perhaps the most destructive of these symptoms is the type of paranoia that focuses on those most dear to the sufferer. There is little hope of resuming a normal lifestyle and previously valued relationships if sufferers continue to hear the voices of loved ones criticizing them and can do nothing about this but try in between times to believe they may be mistaken. This was what was happening to Pat and it was during a more confident phase that she suddenly felt able to confide and explain that her parents sometimes still talked critically to each other about her but she was puzzled as well as hurt because they seemed able to do this without moving their lips! Often when she glanced at them indignantly after they had said something unkind, she noted they were seemingly reading a book or newspaper or watching the television without any sign of also holding a conversation. Such is the strength and force of an auditory hallucination that this intelligent young woman was puzzled and hurt, but only fleetingly wondered if she was again hearing voices.

This was the turning point for Pat when she confided what was happening to her and as a result of the insight gained by all, it was arranged that the young woman would always challenge her mother and father if she believed they were talking about her. They, in turn, would *always* respond honestly to this openness and would encourage their daughter to talk with them about how she was feeling. They would also remind her yet again that as a family they had never made a habit of discussing each other in a disparaging way and that nothing had changed.

In practice, many a happy evening of playing cards, chatting, or watching television was ruined for these parents by an anguished '*What* did you say?' from a suddenly distraught daughter. The parents tried not to show their distress – and this was not always possible – but Pat very gradually *learned to distrust her senses rather than her loved ones.* She would go to bed reassured yet again by their genuine response to her agitated queries. Her parents, however, often had a disturbed night following the realization that their apparently well and normal daughter was still being tortured by the symptoms of paranoia. This process went on for two long years, but the gaps between each incident were lengthening all the time.

It may be clear that this sort of approach is hard work for those closest to the sufferer and sometimes quite depressing. It is so much easier to look at a seemingly recovered relative and persuade oneself that all is well. Only those who have the courage to face up honestly to the lingering nightmare experiences of such individuals will persevere with this approach, but it will eventually prove more rewarding than pretending all is well when in fact this is not the case.

To sum up, this stage of reality testing starts when the sufferer is becoming well enough sometimes to doubt the reality of false messages being received from distorted perceptions and delusional ideas. At this point, sufferer and carer(s) may decide to enter into a contract which involves both parties in the following agreement:

(i)  Every time the sufferer has strange ideas or feelings caused, for example, by intrusive thoughts or by hearing voices, he or she will immediately question the carer(s) as to the authenticity of such ideas.

(ii)  The carer(s) will respond by being completely honest and will find time there and then to discuss the idea as fully as is necessary to reassure or calm the sufferer.

Challenging an almost overwhelming conviction and voicing one's doubts in this way is not at all easy for sufferers and the contract will only be fulfilled if their courage and honesty is met by an equally responsible attitude in the carer(s). This may be difficult to achieve every time, but persevering with this will be immeasurably more positive and rewarding than the more common pitfalls of either colluding with the sufferer (from fear, embarrass-ment or the 'anything for a peaceful life' syndrome) or contradicting or ridiculing strange statements.

Reality testing should provide a safe environment in which to admit to and share unpleasant or frightening ideas caused by symptoms of the illness. Happily, such dedication from others will be amply rewarded by a growing awareness of what it really means to experience this illness from within and by watching a loved one gaining real insight and strength.

Although we have referred to informal carers throughout this second stage of reality testing, this supportive work can be provided by a trusted professional or other worker, particularly where there is no family support. The worker can meet regularly with the sufferer and encourage open discussion of doubts and any strange phenomena which may have still been occurring. Although this will not be so effective as challenging one's experiences at the time they are happening, it will be very much more productive than firmly encouraging sufferers to talk 'positively' about their health (a common practice which reflects widespread denial that we are really dealing with a serious illness). We all need to be able to confide in another person and this has to be particularly true for those individuals whose very senses can let them down. Sufferers will not be helped to get a firm grasp of reality if they have to 'live a lie' all the time.

## (3) Just Checking!

For Pat, the third stage of reality testing was all about those 'off days' when sufferers still feel vulnerable and have the occasional shadowy symptom which they need to be able to discuss openly.

Similarly, there are times when well recovered sufferers still need to seek reassurance about fleeting fears and worries, never quite sure whether or not such fears and worries fall within the range of 'normality'. It can be helpful to be reminded that everyone has these concerns. It may be just the extent of the anxiety which is greater than 'normal' and if this is the case then reassurance will be all the more welcome.

Sometimes, sufferers may be plagued by undermining incidents or sensations which are very upsetting. It can be wonderfully reassuring to discover these are nothing more than lingering symptoms which other sufferers have also experienced. This in turn can offer opportunities for finding ways to cope with these experiences until they eventually wane with the illness. Contact with other sufferers can enhance such opportunities and in Chapter 12 we look at a special kind of groupwork which makes good use of reality testing and the sharing of coping mechanisms.

All in all, then, reality testing is about sharing one's experiences with trusted others and so finding ways to determine exactly what is real and what is fantasy. This gradual acquisition of in-depth insight can be a valuable stand-by in times of stress and threatened relapse. It can also greatly improve a sufferer's quality of life.

Let's now look at another strategy which, like reality testing, can be taken over and managed by sufferers and carers once it has been initiated by service providers:

## Medication 'on Demand'

It is a feature of this illness, although largely unrecognized at the present time, that levels of medication frequently need minor adjustment. Some individuals who keep really well do so because they have doctors who are happy for their potentially stable patients to keep a small supply of extra tablets available for use at times when they feel vulnerable.

I have never known this arrangement cause any problems, because, as we have seen, it is an inherent part of this illness that sufferers are reluctant to admit to a need for medication. In fact, non-compliance over drug treatment or withdrawal of the medication are probably the most frequent cause of relapse. It is only when the illness wanes and insight is gained that sufferers begin really to appreciate the role of their medication in their recovery. At this point, having access to extra medication can protect them when they are feeling particularly vulnerable or when they are having an 'off day' and experiencing shadowy symptoms which may flare up in a very short time.

This used to happen to Sally, whose perceptions of what was happening around her could change within minutes and play havoc with her life within a matter of hours. Rescue on such occasions depended on her finding the courage to seek help and on this being available immediately. She only came really to believe in her medication once she was free to test out its effect each time these traumatic symptoms returned. Eventually she learned that if she took extra tablets immediately, as she had been advised, then the symptoms waned within half-an-hour or so, rather than steadily worsening as they had in the past.

Making this invaluable discovery took a long time because first Sally had to fight her innate resistance to taking extra tablets at all, let alone at times when her paranoid ideas were returning and persuading her that it was not an illness that was causing her distress. Eventually, she had to find out for herself what the medication did for her in these circumstances and, when she did, this was far more convincing than anything she had ever learned from anyone else. It has also given her real confidence to know that she can now protect herself if and when these symptoms threaten to return.

I first heard about this practical approach in the early 1980s when a leading psychiatrist mentioned in a lecture how one of his patients, a young mother, had survived a two hour delay in a motorway service station during which her twin babies screamed at her throughout. She was still exhausted following their recent birth and at one point in the long journey she suddenly remembered his advice to take an extra tablet when she felt vulnerable. This approach made sound sense then and has done so on each occasion I have come across it since. It acknowledges that most sufferers continue to have 'off days' when their symptoms threaten and undermine them. They, like the rest of us, fare better and grow in confidence if they can feel they are in control of their own lives.

What other strategies has Sally found help her to stay well?

## A Positive Lifestyle

Sally believes that it is essential to work towards achieving a regular sleep pattern and for her this has resulted from eating a healthy diet and getting regular exercise; preferably walking, as this involves spending time out in the fresh air each day. It also helped her to find some incentive for getting up at a reasonable time each morning.

Once this sort of routine has been achieved, then Sally recommends taking up an activity such as part-time classes at a local college and, if possible, attending a centre or club for people who have had to cope with similar problems. She puts it this way:

> 'You need what I call a *sane place*, a place where you don't have to pretend all the time. It should be a place where you can share your concerns with other people *who have been there* and listen to theirs. It should be a place where you can relax and feel you *belong*, somewhere, in fact, where you can get everything back into its right perspective!'

## Diet

Sally has made reference to a 'healthy diet' and this is a subject which I have dealt with in some detail in a previous book. *Schizophrenia: A Fresh Approach**
deals with specific food intolerances sometimes associated with this type of

---

* The book is no longer on sale in bookshops but the revised edition is available in public libraries and from the National Schizophrenia Fellowship, the Schizophrenia Association of Great Britain and the Schizophrenia Association of Ireland, 4 Fitzwilliam Place, Dublin 2.

illness and also with the sort of diet I recommend, together with appropriate recipes.

There is a pronounced tendency amongst some schizophrenia sufferers to choose sweet and stodgy snacks in preference to proper meals. These usually consist of refined carbohydrates such as white flour, white rice, sugar, chocolate and ice-cream.

There seems to be little doubt that these individuals do better on a balanced diet and that eating sweet stodgy foods seems merely to promote a craving for more of the same; it also escalates the fluctuation of the body's blood-sugar levels and this affects mood and raises anxiety levels. We have already mentioned this craving and the 'fast and furious' eating habits of a considerable number of sufferers.

There has been persisting interest in theories over the past forty years that a small number of sufferers may well have a wheat gluten intolerance. Dohan, who initiated interest in this subject, has suggested that a fault in the permeability of the gut walls might allow food-derived neuro-active peptides to get into the brain cells.[2] At least two pieces of research support this kind of theory,[3][4] and may also be borne out by the common incidence of gut and bowel disorders in sufferers and their relatives. There can be no doubt at all that sufferers who exhibit this type of eating habit can gain from cutting right down on these stodgy and sweet foods and changing to a more balanced diet which emphasizes protein, fruit and vegetables. They will enjoy an added bonus of controlling any weight-gain associated with taking neuroleptic drugs.

## Making a Routine For Oneself

Stephen shares Sally's faith in getting oneself into a daily routine and explains how he went about gradually achieving this:

> 'It seemed like a long way back to good health and there is a continuing need for patience and determination. The things I found most helpful can be summed up as follows:
>
> (1) Staying in touch with family
>
> (2) Setting personal goals
>
> (3) Settling into a routine
>
> (4) Occupying oneself as much as possible
>
> (5) Eating well.

Staying in touch with my family has helped me; they know me as well as anyone! Setting personal goals and settling into a routine have been most relevant to my gradual recovery which was hampered by the feelings of almost overwhelming apathy and lethargy so typical of this illness. Some days I had no energy at all and could not be bothered to wash, shave or dress properly. Finally, I went back to "square one" and set myself the goal of just cleaning my teeth once a day, every day at least – and there were times I didn't want to do even that! Eventually, I graduated to making sure I was tidy and clean every day before tackling anything else – at last I was settling into a routine which in turn helped me start to get on with my life.

I have found persevering with hobbies and interests useful and that occupational therapy can work. Accept help and be patient. As you become stronger and more motivated, don't waste your time on things that aren't suitable; I have learned to be selective! The illness makes concentrating notoriously difficult; I have found that writing can be easier than trying to read and that listening to music can be easier than watching television. I have also found it important to treat oneself to simple pleasures that provide something to look forward to.

If living alone and lacking experience as a cook, then eating well can be achieved by again adopting a routine; I learned to make sure that I had one good meal a day and then ate out of tins or tucked into a bowl of cereal, the rest of the time. It is a good idea to accept all invitations to eat with family or friends!'

This is sound advice; Stephen struggled for a long time before things started to work out for him, but the turning point came when he at last felt he was in control of his own life.


## Asking For Help

Stephen has one further piece of advice which is endorsed by other sufferers contributing to this book:

'One other lesson I have learned along the way is to never be afraid to ask for help; others may not immediately notice a troubled mind the way they can see a broken leg. It is important *to take responsibility for staying well* by being prepared to seek and accept help when this is needed.'

As we have already noted, this is a vitally important matter. As sufferers become more vulnerable, so they find it harder to seek help; before very long it can be too late. Overcoming this reluctance to admit to one's own vulnerability is common; human beings tend to deny illness in themselves, whatever the condition. In schizophrenia, failure to acknowledge this and a threatened return of symptoms can be disastrous.

## Thinking Positive

The road to recovery in this illness can be long and progress can be so slow that it may not be very obvious to the sufferer. Pat came to terms with this by learning to take each day as it comes. She recommends new sufferers to:

> 'Try keeping a diary. When discouraged by setbacks, look back again to the early days after the diagnosis and congratulate yourself on any real progress made.'

This approach can help some of those individuals who are really doing well but cannot appreciate this because it is happening so slowly. Recalling how they were coping twelve months earlier can put things more into perspective. Similarly, it can lead to a useful exercise deciding what they would like to be achieving in twelve months' time. This brings us to one more important strategy:

## Stretching One's Potential

I have seen too many sufferers unwittingly set up to fail. This frequently occurs when those trying to help them are anxious to provide a routine for them without realizing that this has to evolve gradually on the sort of step-by-step basis that Stephen has described. Most will then need us to make sure they do not eventually settle for too little for themselves. Some make good progress and then find themselves in a rut, lacking the confidence or incentive to move forward. This is not conducive to a continued recovery and they should be encouraged to set themselves attainable goals and to resist the temptation to 'sit back on their laurels' when it all suddenly seems to be too much effort.

This really amounts to being ready to move on each time the previous step has become routine. An example of this might be gradually increasing the number of hours or days spent at a day centre. Just two days a week might be all the individual can cope with initially, finding this quite exhausting and needing to recuperate on the other days. As these two days becomes quite routine, then a third day can be attempted. At first, this extra day may be almost overwhelmingly tiring, as were the first two days originally and a lot of encouragement will be needed. Eventually, the three days will become routine. At this point, the individual might want to take on a fourth day or, possibly, consider attempting a social activity involving a regular evening out each week. Perhaps the next milestone will be a few hours' voluntary work at the weekend or, possibly, a second evening out.

This sort of step-by-step programme will do wonders for some individuals with lingering feelings of apathy and lethargy. They will need constant encouragement to take the next step each time but this should not be contemplated until observers can see that the existing programme is no longer tiring. Several of my clients have called this a 'stretching process' and its success relies on a partnership between sufferers and carers. As time goes on, the individual recognizes the time for the next move forward and will also be starting to have definite ideas on what sort of move this should be. At this point, everyone is winning!

## What To Tell

This is one of the 'evergreen' problems of everyday life with this illness. What does one tell other people?

What does a young male sufferer trying to enjoy a drink in a pub, for instance, reply to someone who says 'what do you do?'. We live in a society which makes instant assessments of people by finding out about their work. I used to be asked for advice on this matter over and over again but anxiety about this has eased a little with the growing unemployment figures; it no longer raises eyebrows if the same young man says 'Well, I'm out of work'. A sufferer then has to consider how to answer the next question, possibly 'Oh I see; what did you used to do?'. Nevertheless, it is not too difficult to work out some sort of innocuous reply, particularly if one's been to college and can start talking about former and present *plans* rather than *reality*!

Again, what should sufferers say about their lifestyle when they meet potential new friends? Perhaps nothing, but this is not easy. I well remember a seemingly confident male client leaping aside from a group of people standing in the grounds of a day hospital and calling out to a passer-by who stopped to greet him, 'Oh, you didn't know I'm working here now, did you?' Everyone looked suitably surprised, but no-one let him down.

The perennial question remains 'what and when shall I tell my new friend?' It is has been my experience that it is in the interests of most sufferers, and probably all, to tell as little as possible initially. People who suffer from other conditions rarely feel compelled to share their medical history with all comers; their medical history is personal and for them to share only if this might start to matter in the context of their relationship with the other person. It is the same with schizophrenia. If there is a real or urgent need for explanations early on in a relationship, then words such as 'depression' and 'nervous breakdown' can be a part of a schizophrenic illness but they do not have the same connotations as 'schizophrenia' for someone who may only have heard horror stories about this illness. It is rarely a good idea for sufferers to share the whole truth until the other person has had a real opportunity to get to know them first. This is important; many individuals have come to terms with schizophrenia because it has been associated with a friend they have learned to like and respect.

As a rule, this sort of advice seems to work in a sufferer's best interests and is justified when we hear so many instances of individuals being deserted in the middle of an evening after an untimely confidence to a near-stranger or valued new 'friend'. Sometimes they will be let down anyway; some 'friends' will not be able to accept the implications of a sufferer's medical history and others will be persuaded by an anxious family to end the friendship. Fortunately, there are many examples of a more positive outcome, given that the sharing of the truth was not too hurried.

These, then, are some of the strategies used by the sufferers, carers and service providers who have contributed to this book. The last we shall be considering here – a special kind of groupwork – needs the whole of the next chapter to itself.

## CHAPTER 12

# Needs Based Groupwork

As we have noted, individuals who have had a schizophrenic illness particularly value 'one-to-one' relationships and it is through these that we can provide a lifeline for a recovering sufferer. This approach can be an enabling one that is rewarding for sufferers and those working with them but we must be careful that it does not lead to over-dependency which will do nothing to boost a damaged self-esteem nor improve social skills.

If the individual is to continue to benefit from a 'one-to-one' casework relationship, then this should eventually provide a stepping-stone to other relationships and to normal socializing. During the 1980s, as I worked more closely with sufferers and their families, I became increasingly sceptical about the value of a continuing 'one-to-one' working relationship as each seemed eventually to reach a point where there was no further development and growth; it was as though the relationship was so 'comfortable' that it precluded any need to stretch out to others. These were the limitations of this approach as I came to see them:

(1) It cannot take away the feeling of isolation; of being different and 'the only one' to have had this nightmare experience; to have had this stigmatized illness.

(2) It encourages feelings of dependency on the worker, which cannot help repair a damaged self-esteem.

(3) The relationship continues to be a lifeline, instead of a stepping-stone.

(4) This intensive work is uneconomical use of time and scarce resources, thus severely limiting numbers who can be helped.

## What About Groupwork?

For some time I had wondered about the potential of groupwork at some stage in the individual's recovery, but was aware of the frustrated attempts in this direction of mental health workers everywhere. All would confirm that this client population do not take kindly to groups and rarely persevere with them. Moreover, I knew sufferers who had gone to quite extreme lengths to avoid being in the right place at the right time if groupwork was provided in hospital. Similarly, it was rare to find professionals using groupwork as a specific tool in the treatment of this type of illness. A search through the copious literature on schizophrenia will confirm that little, if any, work is now attempted in this direction. Why should this be the case? A quick look at the basic concepts of the groups in common use might help us to answer that question:

(1) THE PASSIVE LEADERSHIP GROUP is the type of groupwork most frequently found in a psychiatric setting, with the leader playing a passive and observing role. Members initiate any interaction in the group. If none of these is prepared to break the silence, then this may well continue for long periods, even for the duration of the session.

(2) THE ANALYTIC GROUP's main task is to involve members in searching within themselves and their life experience, with the help of the group and its leader, for the origins of their problem and an understanding of this.

(3) THE ENCOUNTER GROUP's basic concept is that growth and change will be promoted by experiential learning. Everyday inhibitions may be challenged and boundaries become less clear as members are encouraged to relax and trust one another whilst taking part in various exercises, sometimes of a physical nature, within the group.

These admittedly brief and over-simplified observations should nevertheless provide clues as to why schizophrenia sufferers have a pronounced tendency to avoid participation when groupwork is offered them. If we pause and consider for a moment the experiences of a psychotic nightmare and the legacy of problems this can bring in its aftermath, we might expect a recovering sufferer to have to cope with:

(1) A sense of isolation and feeling 'the only one' who has had these experiences

(2) Feelings of guilt and worthlessness

(3)  Heightened anxiety and self-consciousness

(4)  Profound confusion escalated by inadequate knowledge of what has happened

(5)  Lingering symptoms, making it difficult to keep a grasp on reality

(6)  A fear of being with other people because of difficulties in communicating.

Let's now take a second look at the groupwork which is commonly used in psychiatry:

*Passive leadership groups* have no structure, so they can be neither 'safe' nor predictable, making them the last place that some-one recovering from an acute breakdown is likely to be able to relax or learn. Potentially long silences serve to increase feelings of self-consciousness, to escalate anxieties and any paranoid ideas whilst providing no relief from an overactive mind. Meanwhile, although these long silences may not concern sufferers with negative symptoms, neither will they do anything to engage their attention in any way.

*Analytic-type groups* are similarly unsuited to the needs of schizophrenia sufferers. At worst, anything which can be construed as probing is now widely recognized as being dangerous for them. At best, even an innocuous sounding contribution (usually provoked by an anxiety to conform with the norms of the group) can cause later anguish and feelings of guilt. Indignant sufferers refer to groups where 'things are dragged out of you' after such experiences.

*Encounter groups* provide even less structure than the others, making many of the rest of us uneasy when we are members ourselves. Any intimacy and/or need for physical contact serve only to aggravate residual confusion over identity and personal boundaries. Such groups can and often do bring on a psychotic episode in a vulnerable sufferer.

All in all, it is not difficult to understand why sufferers decline to attend such groups and become very vulnerable if they have no choice in the matter. It is quite worrying to consider how counter-productive therapy of this kind could be for individuals with this illness. Let's pause for a moment now and consider why they might find a rewarding 'one-to-one' relationship so much more attractive:

The 'one-to-one' approach provides for

(1) a safe and predictable environment

(2) own time as of right

(3) minimal embarrassment and self-consciousness

(4) feelings of trust

(5) feelings of being valued

(6) feelings of reassurance.

Now let's see what happens to these needs in the sorts of groups we have been looking at:

## Some Disadvantages of Typical Groupwork:

(1) Cannot provide a *safe and predictable environment*; there are no clear boundaries

(2) Cannot provide *own time* as of right, unless members are prepared to offer something which will demand the group's attention

(3) Escalates feelings of *embarrassment* and *self-consciousness*

(4) Silences and raised anxiety heighten feelings of *paranoia rather than trust*

(5) Unlikely to provide *feelings of being valued* in a situation where others do not appreciate or understand the potential 'inner world' of schizophrenia

(6) Cannot provide *reassurance* in these circumstances.

It seemed quite clear at this point in my search why sufferers were neither willing nor ideal subjects for groupwork. Nevertheless, I was becoming increasingly interested in the potential of starting up some kind of *peer groups* for this client population.

There was no evidence of any such work being carried out because of the denial surrounding this diagnosis. Groupworkers I spoke to did not want to know about the diagnosis of their clients and they did not believe that people would come to a group for schizophrenia sufferers as this would immediately advertise their diagnosis to others. However, I could not see that successful groupwork could be undertaken with sufferers unless the groupleader was aware of their diagnosis and its implication. Neither did I feel that we could assume that sufferers would not take up a resource for this sort of reason, if it met their needs.

## Peer Groups

These groups can provide a powerful medium for growth and change because they cater for a membership with a potential bond and I suspected they could be ideal where schizophrenia was the common bond. As we know, peer groups are a popular and successful method of intervention. Health professionals frequently offer them to clients trying to overcome addictions, to clients with eating disorders and to clients with conditions such as diabetes which involves coming to terms with a new lifestyle and learning to cope with problems thrown up by the diagnosis. Not only can members gain from the counselling skills and expertise of the therapist, but they can share their own experiences and methods of coping, whilst providing moral support for each other. I believed that this sort of approach would be particularly relevant in an illness such as schizophrenia which causes its victims to feel alienated by extraordinary experiences that are often incomprehensible to others. I suspected that this sort of group had real potential for helping the victims of this illness and could:

(1) Break down feelings of isolation and alienation, taking away feelings of being 'the only one'

(2) Bring a sense of 'belonging' by becoming a member of an 'in-group' of peers

(3) Improve self-esteem as feedback from peers can be a powerful medium for change

(4) Provide potential and opportunities for forming new relationships

(5) Provide opportunities to learn ways of identifying and coping with residual symptoms and with day-to-day problems arising from these

(6) Provide opportunities to find ways of coping with society's attitude to schizophrenia.

So far, so good; these were the sort of objectives I was aiming for. However, none of these potential advantages would be achieved unless the group could also provide a safe and predictable environment with the attractions of the 'one-to-one' working relationship.

## A Merger

Suddenly it all became clear; there could be no way of guaranteeing that these needs were met without a merger; the groups would represent *a merger* between a 'one-to-one' relationship and a special kind of peer group. With this it might be possible to offer members a safe and predictable environment together with all the potential advantages of interaction with their peers.

This could be achieved by directive leadership and a firm structure in which the leader would engage each member in turn in a 'one-to-one' interaction, whilst encouraging and drawing in other members of the group as appropriate. This would allow for all to have their *own time* and to develop better communication skills via a 'one-to-one' situation *within the group*, providing help and prompting as appropriate. This in turn should allow for the development of feelings of trust and of being valued. Directive leadership and a firm structure could provide an environment which would minimize feelings of anxiety and insecurity. Without this, no learning or growth could take place.

Much to my delight, the theory worked in practice and I have now been running such groups for eight years and others have found, as I have, that this is an exceptionally rewarding way to work with sufferers. Fears that they might shun groups specifically for people with this diagnosis have proved groundless. Some very able sufferers have attended groups for several years at a time. Let's take a look at the basic rules of this method of working:

## Size of Groups

Most groupworkers find 'seven' is the magic number for small groups and Needs Based groups certainly seem most successful with five to eight members. I have found individuals with this illness to be tolerant of larger numbers but this does, of course, restrict the amount of time and attention available for each member. Nevertheless, I have kept the groups 'open' so that we can welcome back any sufferer who might be going through a difficult phase.

## Frequency of Groups

If these are to achieve the worthwhile objective of helping sufferers structure their time, then it is best for the groups to meet on a weekly basis. Larger gaps or changing of days tend to confuse and break the routine, undermining serious attempts by members to discipline themselves into being somewhere at a prescribed time. Clearly, it is essential that the groupleader never lets members down even if the group is at a venue where they anyway attend.

## Length of Groups

An hour is usually long enough for each meeting, although reasonably well-recovered sufferers can cope happily with up to one and a half hours.

I compromise on this and allow for one hour, but warn new members that we might go on for a little longer sometimes. We do that if everyone is involved in something by the end of the hour and there is no inclination to finish immediately.

When working with this client population, I can find no virtue in the common groupwork practice of setting a time for finishing and cutting there and then as a matter of principle, regardless of what might be happening in the group at that time. The aim is to engage sufferers and draw them out of their 'inner world'; it really makes no sense to infer that this is important only if it is achieved at a convenient moment. More important, it would be a folly to bring a group to an abrupt finish if anyone with this type of illness was becoming upset or anxious at that moment; it is essential that this be dealt with first. I have found it a good idea to allow up to one and a half hours for each group and to aim to write up notes immediately afterwards in the extra time that is usually available.

## Duration of Groups

Sometimes I run ongoing groups, in that the majority of the members continue to attend over a long period. However, I have found it best to run each group for an agreed number of sessions, with a short break at Christmas and Easter and a longer break in the summer. This has the advantage of giving the leader an opportunity to meet individually with members, to check on their progress as they each see it, and to make spaces for others when members are ready to move on.

Out of the forty or so sufferers I have worked with in these groups during the past eight years, only a few have opted to leave a group after a first ten week session. It is important here to remember that schizophrenia sufferers often take a period of up to a few years to achieve anything like a real recovery and the premature removal of a resource can undo much of the real work that has been achieved. Even when a member is ready to move on, then I believe it to be desirable that something less formal should be offered such as a social rehabilitation club. This facility may be rejected at the time, but a continuing lifeline has been offered that is sometimes taken up at a later date.

## Selection of Members

These are restricted to individuals who have had a schizophrenic illness or who have the same sort of symptoms, albeit they have been given no diagnosis. Such sufferers may have to cope with residual symptoms or need help with communication skills or be suffering from isolation and a damaged self-image. They must be aware that they have had an illness and wish to find ways of better coping with this.

Mostly, they will be individuals who have suffered with the acute form of schizophrenia, but this does not preclude a chronic sufferer who is motivated to be involved. Several have participated in my groups, which have been all the richer for this. However, it is probably wise to limit their numbers to one or two in a group of seven or more as they will require extra attention from the leader if they are to contribute and if the experience is to be meaningful for them. Similarly, it is not really practicable to attempt to work with an acute sufferer who has uncontrolled psychotic symptoms as this can be disruptive and disturbing for other members and is not likely to be productive for the individual in question either. Having said that, there may well be occasions when a member who is recovering from an acute breakdown will have an 'off day' and be excitable or become more or less detached from reality. So long as this is not a frequent occurrence, the rest of the group will usually rise to the occasion.

## Recruitment of Members

Ideally, prospective members will be familiar to the group leader, who will have had some involvement with them previously. If not, then it will probably suffice to rely on a couple of 'one-to-one' sessions before introducing them to the group, so long as a good rapport has been achieved, with the leader having an understanding of prospective members' own perspective of their problems as well as obtaining details of any significant adverse circumstances in their history and background.

I also make sure that the individual is well primed about what goes on in the group, in order to avoid unnecessary anxiety about 'what happens next?' I mention that new members are not expected to contribute during the first meeting unless they wish to but they are expected to come along to the group at least twice, to make the exercise worthwhile for them and for other members of the group. I then explain the 'rules of the house':

(1) Anything that a member says in the group is confidential and must not be repeated outside. This applies to members and to the leader. However, the latter may be concerned enough about a member's welfare to need to break this rule, but only after discussing this with the individual first.

(2) Each member is expected to make a commitment to the group, attending regularly and remaining for the duration of each meeting (this can be quite an accomplishment for an individual

still in a restless phase) and to refrain from smoking throughout (quite apart from changing health regulations, requests for a light, a cigarette, or an ashtray tend to come at all the wrong times and can be disruptive and off-putting for other members). This latter rule has presented no problems, even with heavy smokers.

Being asked to make a commitment to attend regularly is important when sufferers are needing to structure their everyday lives into some sort of routine. It is also important that all members of the group should feel that each values the experience of the group enough to attend regularly. It has to be a measure of the success of this work that these simple requirements have produced remarkable achievements in terms of regular and punctual attendance that would put most of us to shame. Indeed, they tend to challenge our ideas of lack of motivation in this illness; once their enthusiasm is engaged, the staying power of sufferers can be an example to us all.

### The Venue

I have worked with these groups in such a variety of settings and sizes of room that I have come to believe that this aspect of the environment is not particularly important. However, it is essential that the room in which the group meets affords privacy with freedom from interruption and provides reasonable comfort and warmth.

If there is to be some choice in the matter then ideally the setting will allow for members to wander in up to half an hour before the start of the group (e.g. to allow for the idiosyncrasies of public transport and to provide natural opportunities for socializing) and also provide tea-making facilities for members if they wish to relax together at the end of the group.

### Group Leader

There are several qualities and characteristics that anyone running a Need Based group will need to have and this will become clearer when we later take a look at this method of working. Ideally, leaders will need to have:

(1) A sound knowledge and understanding of this type of illness and the problems this can bring sufferers and carers

(2) An empathic and accepting manner

(3) A real interest in everything that is said in the group together with good observational and recall skills

(4) No problems with being directive.

## Preparation for the Group

It might seem that I have given little emphasis to the material aspect of the environment where the group meets but I would now stress that it is very important to create the right psychological atmosphere from the beginning. Bearing in mind the frantic pace of life for most of us nowadays, I always find it is worth advising a new group leader to allow a few minutes before entering the group; to sit down, to draw a deep breath and to SLOW DOWN, before switching off from the rest of the day's pressures. It can be really helpful to slow oneself down and to make a conscious effort to talk less quickly than usual, carefully weighing each word one speaks. By doing this, the leader can make it easier for all to relax and concentrate on what is going on. As we have seen, sufferers often have trouble keeping pace with all that goes on around them and tend to feel bombarded with stimuli.

It is worth going through this routine before each group and using these few moments to recall the needs that the group is aiming to meet.

## Running a Needs Based Group

In describing the method of working below, I outline this method of working for prospective group leaders in the form of numbered instructions, followed by comments on each as appropriate.

(1) Go into the group at the time it is due to start, with a welcoming smile and a 'hello' that includes everyone present. Aim for informality and the use of first names throughout.

It may be that you will need to introduce a new member at this point. If so, rather than expecting the individual to speak at this stage, you can ask the rest of the group if any members would like to say a few words about themselves to the newcomer (thus giving the latter a chance to relax and encouraging worthwhile social skills in welcoming newcomers and in 'public speaking'). Sometimes there will be no offers and then it should suffice to ask members to just introduce themselves by name.

(2) Focus on each member in turn, starting with anyone looking concerned or catching your attention, for whatever reason, and commence dialogue with this individual. Start with something like 'How are you today?' or 'How have you been feeling since we last met?'

These sort of questions indicate that it is all right to talk about oneself and one's health – a rare luxury for individuals with this illness and one that is usually welcomed.

(3) If the answer produces nothing in particular, follow up with something like 'Have you had any problems/difficulties?' or 'Is anything worrying you?'

These sort of questions indicate that it is all right and appropriate to talk about problems.

(4) If the answer still produces nothing in particular, follow up with something like 'Oh, that's good! Has anything interesting happened to you since the last group?' (thus ensuring this member's 'own time' before moving on).

Just very occasionally a member may for some time avoid bringing anything of real concern to the group, using it as a chance just to talk about things of little consequence to others in the group. In this case, it may be helpful after a couple of such instances next time to rephrase the last question, in other words, 'Has anything happened to you since we last met *which would be relevant to the business of this group?*'

(5) Right from the start of any dialogue taking place, it is important to respond to non-verbal signals in the group, drawing in anyone who is reacting by nodding, or who might have a similar experience or interest. Finally, always come back to the original member (whose 'own time' it is) before moving on to each of the other members in turn.

This is where observation, recall, and knowledge of group members becomes important.

(6) Be careful to encourage all individual contributions with something like 'Oh, I'm glad you brought that up' or 'I think that is an important matter for quite a few people.'

This indicates that you feel the individual's comment is a useful one and so, probably, do others in the group. All attempts by members to be involved should be nurtured by you, thus giving constant feedback that each and every member is valued and has an important contribution to make.

(7) Better still, whenever possible, draw other members in with 'I believe you've been worried about that as well, Harry, haven't you?' or 'I think one or two other members have had that problem – I wonder how they've dealt with it?', glancing round appropriately.

Not only are you indicating to the individual that the original comment was worthwhile but, more important, that others in the group *have been there*. This brings with it feelings of reassurance and may open up opportunities for reality testing if the problem turns out to be a residual symptom, shared by others, rather than an embarrassing reality.

(8) At this point, other members can be drawn in with 'Could you explain how you coped, Tom? Jane might find that helpful' or some such.

Similarly, this approach can open up opportunities for sharing methods of coping.

(9) It is important that the discussion remains structured and interruptions or asides can be dealt with by cheerful comments such as 'One at a time, please', or 'We can come back to you'; any new found confidence in your members may be fragile!

It may be interesting to note at this point that this method of working provides space and time for typically reserved sufferers whilst making boundaries for the minority who might otherwise talk incessantly. Furthermore, it creates opportunities for the latter to talk about matters *brought up by other members* by joining in the discussion when these are raised. In this way, it caters for two of the main problems in groupwork generally; the too passive member and the too volatile member and encourages more appropriate skills in both.

(10) The group proceeds by returning each time to the original member after others have joined in the discussion promoted by that individual, before eventually moving on to the next one. This initial dialogue with each person in turn can take up a whole meeting if the topics raised are of particular interest to members. More usually, the group will move onto other things and to a more general discussion.

This further discussion will need to be 'orchestrated' by the leader at all times *but the subject matter must originate from the members.* I originally fell into the trap of preparing a topic just in case my reserved clients allowed the discussion to die; this turned out to be counter-productive because the group then focused on general topics rather than on themselves and matters of their own choosing. The directive role of the leader should focus on facilitating discussion *which originates from the members.*

(1 1) Before closing each meeting, give all members a chance to bring up anything that has not been dealt with in the group and that is important to them, making it clear that you would welcome this and there is time allowed for it.

Someone will usually take advantage of this offer. However, be careful to 'nip in the bud' individual approaches and 'after-thoughts' *following* the end of the meeting. Something like 'perhaps you'd like to bring that to the next group?' should suffice.

## Some More Comments About the Leader's Role

In this type of groupwork, the leader will be actively involved in what is going on throughout the session, needing to 'join up' the sentences and keeping the conversation afloat. Remember, clients may be handicapped by a crippling 'poverty of speech' in the early days after an acute breakdown and have other difficulties with communicating as well. On top of this, they may be nervous of other people, acutely self-conscious and generally lacking in confidence. The leader will be the link between each person's contributions and for a while this may be very much a 'questions and answers' formula which can be s-t-r-e-t-c-h-e-d as it were into an ongoing exchange.

This is important as the group can be experienced as a series of individual interviews without this constant 'networking'. Constant observation and awareness, particularly of non-verbal signals, are vital if this process is to work. A keen interest in group members and, essentially, a good recall of what they have said in the past will facilitate this networking by bringing others into the discussion when they might otherwise hang back. Most of all, the clear appreciation and valuing of each member's contribution is quickly picked up by the group and this leads to feelings of trust and mutual respect. Furthermore, it sets an example which leads to a total absence of any scapegoating in Needs Based groups, although this a recognized feature in other types of groupwork.

## A Typical Needs Based Group

Usually members will enthusiastically discuss anything important that has happened to them since the last group and any problems they are having. For some, these will be the everyday difficulties presented by the conspiracy of silence and stigma surrounding this illness. For others, their problems will be concerned with a struggle to cope with residual symptoms. One colleague who has worked in Needs Based groups has asked me to stress that some of the revelations that can come up in an established group may be quite unnerving, even shocking, for an uninitiated group leader, An example might be the distressing details of the sort of intrusive thoughts we discussed in the second chapter of this book.

Not only may affected members need to discuss these, they will also need to have reassurance that they are not condemned by the group for having such thoughts; that they are not to blame in any way for these and that others in the group do not believe they would act upon them. It is important for group leaders to think through such matters and how they would deal with any rejecting feelings these might provoke in them.

Similarly, it can be quite unsettling to have a female sufferer suddenly reveal very inappropriate and bizarre sexual ideas and try to cope with one's own and other members' astonished reaction to these.

However, having said that, most groups apply themselves to the predictable problems of individuals trying to cope with everyday issues in this illness. The subjects that come up again and again tend to be as follows:

(1) residual symptoms and reality testing

(2) coming to terms with one's diagnosis and what it means

(3) coming to terms with medication (including a healthy tendency to have a good moan about this on the one hand and to encourage others not to come off it on the other!)

(4) street drugs

(5) having an intimate relationship and the desire for a close partnership with another person rather than a need for this to be necessarily sexual

(6) society's attitudes and the pressure of others' expectations on one to be 'normal'; to have a job, for instance

(7) feelings of guilt and self-blame.

## So What is Happening in Needs Based Groupwork?

Perhaps it is clear that group members are indeed being offered within a group most of the features of a 'one-to-one' approach? The environment is *safe* and *predictable* because it is structured by a leader who is providing the boundaries for the group. They have their *own time*. They feel *valued* because the leader nurtures each and every contribution and this encourages others to do the same. They learn to *trust* because they see that each member is valued. A *lifeline* is still available because the leader can pick up signs of distress or relapse and deal with them as appropriate. Because the atmosphere is congenial to them, most sufferers persevere with the group, taking advantage of the full benefits which Needs Based groupwork can offer. These include the following:

### Lifestyle

- Stimulation, with relief from a tormented mind
- Structuring of time
- Opportunity to make and keep an ongoing commitment
- Opportunity to re-develop powers of concentration
- The setting and achieving of realistic goals.

### Quality of Life

- A sense of 'belonging'
- Raised self-esteem
- Improved communication skills
- Potential to develop new relationships.

### Keeping Well

- Developing good understanding of the illness
- Coming to terms with one's diagnosis
- Opportunities for reality testing
- Sharing ways of coping
- Insight into one's own vulnerability.

Since the advent of Needs Based groups, several colleagues have joined me in training voluntary counsellors in this special type of groupwork, demonstrating that this tool can be successfully shared. We have found considerable enthusiasm amongst fellow professionals and other workers for learning and adopting a method of groupwork that meets the need of a client population notorious for rejecting groups. Workers and sufferers alike seem to find Needs

Based groups rewarding. When I have asked individuals who have attended my groups over periods of several years why they have persevered with them for so long, the same sort of answers tend to come back each time:

'I like the relaxed and caring atmosphere.'

'In this group everyone matters.'

'We always seem to talk about things that are important for me.'

'Information is never dragged out of anyone.'

'The group always seems to know when something is wrong.'

'The group helps everyone assess their "plusses" and "minuses" so we take the next step at the right time.'

'Because we talk fully and openly about schizophrenia in the group, I find I can forget about it most of the rest of the time.'

'This is the only therapy that has ever helped me.'

Finally, one well-educated young woman told me:

'This is the only chance I have to talk about how I feel; it is the only place it's OK to say that I don't feel well today!.'

At the time she said this she had been attending a day care resource for eighteen months where mental health professionals discouraged any reference at all to health matters. She valued her Needs Based group as the only service she was receiving which met her needs *as she saw them*.

We'll stop there, with the clients having the final word on Needs Based groups.

# IV
# A Way Forward

## CHAPTER 13

# Damage Limitation

Throughout this book, we have considered in some detail how service providers can work in partnership with sufferers and their families in order better to meet the needs of those trying to cope with a schizophrenic illness. As we have seen, a Needs Based approach to schizophrenia relies to some extent on quite dramatic change. It relies on a change from crisis intervention to *crisis prevention*. It relies on crisis prevention in an area in which this could remove an enormous financial burden from our health services while minimizing the havoc wrought by a potentially destructive illness. If such a fantasy were to become reality, what sort of changes would have to take place? How could we really limit the damage caused by our existing 'let's wait and see' approach?

## A Damage Limitation Model

This model can be divided into six stages, with some inevitable overlap between each:

Stage 1 - Education and training

Stage 2 - Acknowledgement, diagnosis and treatment

Stage 3 - Explanations

Stage 4 - Keeping Well

Stage 5 - Threatened relapse

Stage 6 - Crisis prevention.

## (1) Education and Training

Effective education and training will provide two bonuses. They will contribute to a changing of attitudes in a society fearful and ignorant about schizophrenia and they should also bring about a more appropriate response to the needs of sufferers and carers than the existing one. Let's first of all consider how we should go about replacing this fear and ignorance:

(i) We must educate society about this illness, starting with 12-year-olds in our schools. Information on psychotic illness could be provided alongside existing educational programmes on drugs/solvents-abuse and AIDS. Similar programmes could be provided for all those who work with young people in schools, colleges, youth clubs, and church groups. Survivors – both sufferers and carers – should be encouraged to take part in and to influence the content of these educational programmes. The government would need to back up local endeavours with health education programmes using the national media and, perhaps, the sort of home mailing schemes with which it is publicizing its 'citizens charter' schemes.

Local and national projects should emphasise two main themes; (a) that schizophrenia can happen to any of us and does in fact affect something like one in every thirty 'ordinary' families in our society, and (b) that we can all contribute to preventing it from becoming a serious problem because it is a *treatable* illness.

(ii) We must do something about the education and training provided for service providers. Rachel Perkins and Sarah Dilks have found, as have my colleagues and I, that there is a dearth of literature

'to which we can refer trainees, those entering the field, and non-professionals who may be involved, concerning the very basic considerations and approaches that may be helpful'

but their own article on working with severely socially disabled people[1] seeks very aptly to start to remedy this. It addresses the real handicaps posed by the symptoms of an illness such as schizophrenia and finds ways to bridge the gap caused by these handicaps. Such an approach might well be very helpful to many trainee health professionals and other service providers going on to work with such clients on a day-to-day basis.

While professional training programmes often omit to consider the experiences of a psychotic illness and the practical problems facing sufferers and carers, the literature continues to abound with fanciful notions such as those in a recently published book which describes schizophrenia as a bold adventure, 'a difficult stepping-stone to the enlightened side of the stream'[2]. Just how many of us would care to join sufferers on this bold adventure which interrupts and aborts the dreams and plans of so many? The trouble with these sort of euphemisms is that they can distract us from our responsibilities to address the urgent problems facing the victims of this illness.

(iii) We must do something to address the attitudes of those professionals who spend more energy seeking to prove that schizophrenia is a myth rather than in addressing the problems it raises. There is an urgent need for more action and less talking in the handling of serious mental illness; if training programmes addressed themselves rather more to the practical everyday problems this produces than to popular academic debate, then perhaps such professionals would find more job satisfaction tackling these problems.

(iv) We must do something to resolve a 'different perception problem' that Heather highlights below:

'During conversation with a Director of Mental Health Services, he told me that family carers, because of their over-involvement, have a different perception to professional carers, and because of this over-involvement, family carers' perception is less likely to be right.

As a professional carer myself, running a busy outpatients department, and as a voluntary co-ordinator of a large carers' group and mother of a sufferer, I have observed that inevitably those closest to the individual are proved to be right in their perception of the problem. Unfortunately this will usually only follow much pain and anguish for the sufferer, their carers and society.

This difference of perception problem *must* be resolved with formal and informal carers working in partnership to the benefit of all concerned.'

We have already seen examples of formal and informal carers working in partnership; in our own needs based approach and in the work carried out by clinical psychologists at All Saints Hospital in Birmingham which has been referred to several times in this book.[3] We could do with a lot more!

Now, on to the second stage, which again relies very much on effective training for the professionals concerned, as we shall see.

## (2) Acknowledgement, Diagnosis and Treatment

This starts with the first calls for help from those watching someone they love sinking into a psychotic nightmare. We have looked at ways in which we can expedite acknowledgement, diagnosis and treatment, but it is rare to find this happening in practice. There is little chance of it happening unless the family GP is aware of the signs which can indicate underlying psychotic symptoms. Unfortunately, although GPs are the gateway to the mental health services, many of them have had very little opportunity to acquire any real knowledge of psychiatry. In 1988, a junior health minister stressed the importance of 'prevention' in mental illness and mentioned the possibility of 'finding ways of helping GPs identify and treat psychiatric problems at any early stage'[4]. I once observed a GP stand up at the end of a lecture on schizophrenia and ask what sort of signs he should look out for? After an embarrassed silence, the experts on the platform ignored the question. This was a shame; this brave man was not the only member in that multi-disciplined audience who would have been delighted to obtain such information.

As we have seen, it is quite common for GPs to take the view that they cannot intervene unless the individual concerned seeks their help, even when families are explaining why this cannot happen. If this is the case, the GP can then make a request for a psychiatrist to make a home visit. This *domiciliary visit* is provided for under the NHS for just such eventualities, but some GPs do not take advantage of this service and most families are unaware of it. Nevertheless, these doctors really have no option but to persevere with finding a quick solution to the problem the family is presenting; it is, after all, a patient on their books who is causing the concern.

Some GPs, however, are quick to react to indications that one of their patients may be developing a psychotic illness but they in turn may be thwarted in this if the psychiatrist who picks up the case worries less about the effects of an untreated psychosis than about the concerns discussed under the heading Diagnosis in Chapter 6. A large survey carried out during the 1980s within the membership of the National Schizophrenia Fellowship revealed that:

> 'in 185 out of 889 first episodes, the GP was not prepared to treat the problem seriously and in another 80 cases, the GP was sympathetic but could not get help from the psychiatric services.'[5]

Thus roughly one third of this sample were hampered in their attempts to get help for a sick relative for the sort of reasons we have been discussing here. As we noted earlier, the same survey revealed that '161 sufferers obtained no help for their first schizophrenic episode until the police intervened' and this is perhaps not surprising. Clearly, this situation has to change and the two factors which will be most influential here will be (a) improved training facilities for GPs and (b) a climate in which they and the doctors who practise psychiatry will be more concerned with avoiding unnecessary delays in treating this illness than with waiting helplessly for the inevitable crisis which will finally demand a response.

In achieving this, appreciation would be needed that some sort of half-way diagnosis would be required, which would side-step requirements of DSM III to allow for six months of symptoms before diagnosing schizophrenia. Otherwise, any attempts at prevention will be sabotaged from square one.

Once again, the next stage of this model relies on service providers having an adequate education and training in this illness.

## (3) Explanations

As we have noted, explanations are quite significantly absent in many cases of schizophrenia.

(i) Families complain they have to learn by trial and error[6] and it seems that a considerable number of carers never receive adequate explanations about this illness.[7] Some of these latter have highlighted the sort of explanations they consider to be a priority in coping with schizophrenia and we would do well to note these.

Explanations – rather than platitudes – should start at the time of a first call for help. As soon as the illness is acknowledged, albeit tentatively, then families should be fully informed about schizophrenia and the vulnerability this implies. This can be achieved in a positive manner, with emphasis on the treatability of this illness and the need to minimize any damage which might be inflicted by further episodes.

(ii) First-time sufferers very often have little understanding of what has happened to them and they don't really stand a chance unless they are given full explanations about this. As we have noted, this can be carried out in several stages, incorporating reassurance, reality testing and full explanations.

The next stage of this model relies on these full explanations having been made available to sufferers and families as a matter of course.

## (4) Keeping Well

(i)   Sufferers can only keep well if they have insight into their illness
      and into their vulnerability; this will rely on adequate explanations
      and on opportunities to test reality and to gain insight, preferably
      during their first bout of the illness.

The insight involves four vital components; (a) recognition that what has
happened to them has been due to a treatable illness; (b) understanding that
there is a continuing risk of further breakdown; (c) appreciation of the sort
of lifestyle which can lessen this risk; (d) understanding of the pros and cons
of taking medication and the role it has in the maintained recovery of many
sufferers. A fifth component for many sufferers, and one which may come
much later, is acceptance of their need to take this medication indefinitely if
they are to avoid further breakdown.

Sufferers are more likely to protect themselves at all times if they have a
family who support them in this. Similarly they are more likely to overcome
an occasional reluctance to continue to take medication if they have this
support or if they can discuss such matters in a supervised group situation,
such as that described in Chapter 12.

(ii)  Other important factors in keeping well will be those which affect
      the individual's quality of life; in other words, adequate income
      and accommodation, a rewarding lifestyle and a supportive social
      network. We have already touched on ways that society can work
      towards providing for these.

## (5) Threatened Relapse

The 'revolving door' syndrome provides all the evidence we need that a
substantial number of sufferers will continue to relapse regularly unless we
become alert to the first signs of relapse and intervene immediately. Probably
the most important subject we have discussed in this book has been the
realization during the past decade or so that we can do just that; we can
intervene in the short period during which sufferers recognize that they need
help. Furthermore, we know from the work carried out by Max Birchwood,
Jo Smith and their colleagues at All Saints Hospital in Birmingham[8], that
fifty-nine per cent of relatives recognized the early warning signs a month
before relapse and seventy-five per cent recognized them at least two weeks
before relapse. If we are to 'stop the rot' and prevent all the waste and
deterioration in this illness, then we must take notice of those closest to
sufferers when they sense that things are going wrong and seek our help.

There are three ways in which we can seek to protect sufferers from relapse:

(i)   All the carers involved with sufferers must liaise with them and with each other, being aware of the signs of relapse in each individual; a good example is the work carried out by the team in Birmingham[9] following the completion of the above research.

(ii)  All carers must liaise closely if they are to avoid making changes which will actually expedite such relapse. As we noted in Chapters 4, 6 and 7, it is dangerous practice to reduce or withdraw medication without recourse to those closest to the sufferer. More generally, serious attempts to tackle the 'revolving door' syndrome should take note of the effects of continuously reducing medication throughout a sufferer's recovery.

(iii) Many stable sufferers manage to keep very well by taking extra medication whenever they are troubled by symptoms. As we noted earlier, this option, preferably combined with a regular depot injection, can enable sufferers to do something for themselves when they feel vulnerable and allows them to feel they are in control of their own lives.

## (6) Crisis Prevention

So what must we do if the relapse has passed the stage when a sufferer will accept help? It is at this point that everyone has a duty to become *proactive* rather than reactive. It is at this point that we can choose whether to let sufferers sink into a downward spiral of despair and torment, together with all those closely involved, or we can make use of the Mental Health Act 1983 to admit them *in the interests of (their) health*[10]. We do not have to wait for them to demonstrate that they are a danger to themselves or others; we just have to bear in mind that they have an illness which (a) involves an inevitable decline at this point and which (b) is now believed to be 'biologically toxic' as well as 'demoralizing and stigmatizing'.[11]

The only possible objections to taking this action can be those concerned with civil rights. We live in a climate at the moment which emphasizes what Kathleen Jones calls 'negative rights' rather than 'positive rights'. These latter she describes as the rights to a decent quality of life, to a home, to a job, and to care and treatment when we need it. As she claims, these rights have been ignored in favour of negative rights:

> '*not* to be categorized as mentally ill, *not* to be committed to hospital, and *not* to receive treatment.'[12]

It is in this climate that we hear every day that very sick individuals are 'not sectionable', with several more time-consuming visits made before this decision is amended. It seems that many professionals working with the mental health legislation are more concerned with these negative rights than with good practice and with knowing their law. And yet they blame this law for their decisions to take no action.

It is also in this 'civil liberties' climate that we hear nothing about the rights of those closest to the sick individual; whether they be family, friends or neighbours. It is a very puzzling concept that not only should we accept the moral grounds for emphasizing negative rights for people who are ill but that we should also accept that others in the community have no rights at all. This is scarcely the way forward for community care.

Similarly, as we have noted in a previous chapter, every time there is an attempt to amend the mental health legislation, those who oppose this also claim that it is the *interpretation* of the law which is at fault, not the law itself. This is an accurate assessment of the situation which nevertheless takes us nowhere because it does not seem to lead to any improvements in interpretation.

The climate which emphasizes negative rights also allows the supporters of such ideas to claim the 'moral high ground'. It is so easy to defend a stand which protects individuals from being 'incarcerated' on the whim of a 'selfish family' or an 'intolerant society'. *Sectioning* has become an obscene word for some professionals. Many of us working with schizophrenia know GPs, psychiatrists and ASWs who will go to enormous lengths to avoid using the mental health legislation to section individuals who are desperately ill.

In order that we may consider using a Damage Limitation model such as this one, I would challenge these professionals to consider the following:

If you have a basic knowledge of schizophrenia, this will include an understanding that:

(i) there is an ever present risk of relapse

(ii) when this threatens, there is a short period during which sufferers recognize their need for help

(iii) this being so, this is our last opportunity to intervene during this threatened relapse with the individual's agreement

(iv) if we miss this opportunity, then deterioration and eventual relapse become inevitable unless we intervene

(v) as such, we have no alternative but to respond when those closest to them claim that sufferers are now out of touch with reality about their illness and are becoming psychotic. We have no alternative because this is now our one remaining opportunity to intervene and to stop the inevitable decline which will follow because of the diagnosis.

Failure to act at (v) will merely lead to further trauma and breakdown, with all the damage this involves to sufferers and those closest to them and at enormous expense to our health services. In short, if the system lets schizophrenia sufferers down at (iii), that is, at the first signs of relapse, then we have a responsibility to do something about this.

We need to appreciate that 'masterly inactivity' does not give us the 'moral high ground'; it merely demonstrates that we are not equipped or prepared to stop the potential devastation of this illness. This in turn means that some of the professionals working with the mental health legislation end up intervening long after everyone else in the community recognizes the need for this and long after they can claim to be protecting the interests of the sufferer, or anyone else for that matter. Worse, in some instances, they may even turn away with excuses that the resultant behaviour of a delusioned individual is 'bad' not 'mad'.

Such practice will be unacceptable as well as wasteful if we all start to interpret the law correctly and if involved professionals become accountable for their decisions. Both of these recommendations are, of course, implicit in this model.

## Summing Up

These, then, are the components of a Damage Limitation model which could pave the way for us to combat the suffering and the enormous costs of this suffering for our society. It complements the principles of a Needs Based Approach in which we have sought

(1) to obtain a sound knowledge base about what happens in schizophrenia

(2) to obtain a real appreciation of what this means for sufferers and their families or other carers

(3) to work in partnership with sufferers and carers, continuing to identify their needs and attempting to find ways of meeting these needs

(4) to identify and develop tools which can contribute to meeting these needs

(5) to share the experience and expertise gained from this partnership with other service providers.

The model also provides a framework in which such an approach can be used to maximum effect. Why don't we try turning this fantasy into reality? We could start by acknowledging where the real expertise lies at present.

## Schizophrenia: The Experts

There are a small band of specialists who are largely ignored at present. These are the sufferers who eventually make a lasting recovery, *having first gained insight into their illness.*

At the present time, there is a pronounced tendency for the mentally ill to be represented by what have become known as 'professional users' who claim that there is no such thing as a serious mental illness. Some make the paradoxical claim that they are 'survivors', whilst denying the concept of mental illness. They do this by saying they are survivors of the psychiatric system rather than survivors of a mental illness. They refer to having suffered from 'emotional distress', which could be quite valid if they then went on to represent others who are 'emotionally distressed'. They don't; they are accepted as representatives of the silent majority of those with a serious mental illness; those who cannot escape the reality of this and who are not helped by volatile claims that mental illness is a myth. If these 'survivors' have little in common with sufferers who have experienced a classic cluster of symptoms which are responsive to prescribed drugs, how much less can these articulate individuals hope to represent the 'chronic sufferers' whose illness has changed their personalities and lives tragically and beyond recognition?

If we are really interested in 'user' involvement, let's find ways of making sure that all parties are properly represented; there are articulate individuals who can represent the cause of those with a schizophrenic illness but they will not be bringing with them messages that serious mental illness is something dreamt up by others.

On a similar theme, The World Schizophrenia Fellowship has pointed out the recent trend in which:

> 'professionals cross discipline boundaries and become 'schizophrenia specialists', knowledgeable and helpful in many areas'[13]

There certainly does seem to be a small but dedicated band of professionals and other workers worldwide who have applied themselves to acquiring considerable knowledge in a subject surrounded with so much ignorance.

Perhaps the time has come when we need to resort to tapping this wealth of expertise and listen carefully to recovered sufferers, to carers who have learned to live with schizophrenia and to specialist workers – and to let them demonstrate how schizophrenia can be handled in a way that will stop all the unnecessary suffering and the financial burden which goes with it?

Let's give the last word to one such expert, Tina, who suggests we bear in mind her comments in Chapter 5 and start afresh, tackling schizophrenia with DETERMINATION, DEDICATION and a little MEDICATION.

# REFERENCES

## INTRODUCTION

1. Liz Sayce, 'Over-simple arguments and dangerous reductionism', *Community Care*, 19th March 1992.
2. 'Britain's Offbeat Psychiatrist', Newsweek, P 16, November 1st, 1982, quoted in E Fuller Torrey, *Surviving Schizophrenia*, revised edition 1988, (Harper & Row, New York)

## CHAPTER 1

1. Quoted in preface of Dexter, G and Walsh, *Psychiatric Nursing Skills – A patient-centred approach*, London: Croom Helm 1986, introduced as a 'core text for psychiatric nurses in training' which makes two fleeting references to schizophrenia.
2. CCETSW Paper No. 19.25, 'Refresher Training for Approved Social Workers', February 1990.
3. Richard Wyatt, 'Neuroleptics and the Natural Course of Schizophrenia', *Schizophrenia Bulletin*, Volume 17, No 2, 1991.
4. Reported by Mr Patrick Thompson, MP, in House of Commons debate on Mentally Ill People, *Community Care*, 1st February 1989.
5. John Wing,'Schizophrenia and Its Management in the Community', p.18, published by the National Schizophrenia Fellowship from an article in Psychiatric Medicine, New York, 1977 quoted in Gwen Howe, *Schizophrenia: A Fresh Approach*, David & Charles, revised edition, 1990.
6. Johnstone, E, *et al. The Northwick Park Study of First Episodes of Schizophrenia*, Part I – 'Presentation of the illness and problems relating to admission', *British Journal of Psychiatry*, 148 (1986), 115–20.
7. Mary Tyler, from an unpublished survey carried out amongst members of the National Schizophrenia Fellowship, 1936.
8. Department of Health booklet, 1992, summarizing the proposals for a health strategy for England, set out in the White Paper, 'The Health of the Nation: A Strategy for Health in England' (1986).
9. Gwen Howe, *The Reality of Schizophrenia*, London: Faber & Faber 1991.
10. Jablensky, A, Sartorius N, Enberg G, Anker M, Korten A, Cooper J, Day R, Bentelsen A, 'Schizophrenia: Manifestations, incidence and course in different

cultures; A World Heath Organization ten country study', *Psychological Medicine* 1992, Supplement 20.

## Chapter 2

1. Carol North, *Welcome Silence*, London: Simon & Schuster, 1987.
2. Anonymous, 'An autobiography of a schizophrenic experience', *Journal of Abnormal & Social Psychology*, 51 (1955) 677–89.
3. *NSF TODAY*, July 1993, reported a death associated with water intoxication in hospital, with extensive information made available at the Inquest.
4. Crow, T, 'Type I and Type II syndromes', *British Journal of Psychiatry*, 137 (1980), 383–6.

## Chapter 3

1. Gwen Howe, *The Reality of Schizophrenia*, London: Faber & Faber 1991, see Chapter 1 – Steven.
2. G Carstairs, D Early, H Rollin, & J Wing, Medical Advisers to the National Schizophrenia Fellowship, *The Bulletin of the Royal College of Psychiatrists*, 9, 3, pp 59–60 (March 1985) quoted in *Schizophrenia: A Fresh Approach*, David & Charles, 1986.
3. Sally Cooper & Gwen Howe, unpublished survey carried out with members of Southend NSF Group, Spring 1993.
4. Julie Barnett, 'SIMON', printed in *NSF TODAY*, November 1993.

## Chapter 4

1. Johnstone, E *et al. The Northwick Park Study of First Episodes of Schizophrenia*, Part I – 'Presentation of the illness and problems relating to admission', *British Journal of Psychiatry*, 148 (1986) 115–20.
2. See, for example, Crow T, *et al. The Northwick Park Study of First Episodes of Schizophrenia*, Part II: 'A randomized controlled trial of prophylactic neuroleptic treatment', *British Journal of Psychiatry*, 148,(1986), 120–7 and Richard Wyatt, 'Neuroleptics and the Natural Course of Schizophrenia', *Schizophrenia Bulletin*, Vol 17, No.2, 1991, 347
3. Sally Cooper and Gwen Howe, unpublished survey carried out with members of Southend NSF Group, Spring 1993.
4. Max Birchwood, Jo Smith, *et al.* 'Predicting relapse in schizophrenia: the development and implementation of an early signs monitoring system using patients and families as observers, a preliminary investigation', *Psychological Medicine*, 1989, 19, 649–656.
5. An NSF sponsored Needs Based Training Study Day, 31st January 1992.
6. *Mental Health Act 1983*, HMSO publication, Part II.

## Chapter 5

1. See Gwen Howe, *The Reality of Schizophrenia*, London: Faber & Faber, 1991, p.152.
2. See (1) above, p.151.
3. See (1) above, p.169.

## Chapter 6

1. Stephanie Cole, *Week's Good Cause*, BBC Radio 4, 2nd January 1994.
2. Gwen Howe, *The Reality of Schizophrenia*, London: Faber & Faber, 1991, p.148.
3. Stromgen, E, 'Changes in the incidence of schizophrenia?', *British Journal of Psychiatry*, 150 (1987), 1–7.
4. Bleuler, M 'The long term course of schizophrenic psychoses' pp 631–6 in *The Nature of Schizophrenia* ed Wynne, Cromwell and Matthysse (New York: Wiley, 1978): his finding that at least 25% of all schizophrenics recover entirely after one breakdown and remain recovered for good is frequently quoted. However, 'recovery' allowed for the persistence of delusions and perceptual disturbance.
5. American Psychiatric Association, *Diagnostic and Statistical Manual of Mental Disorders*, 3rd edition (Washington, DC, 1980).
6. Crow, T, 'The continuum of psychosis and its implications for the structure of the gene', *British Journal of Psychiatry*, 149 (1986), 419.
7. Sally Cooper and Gwen Howe, unpublished survey carried out with Southend NSF Group members, Spring 1993.
8. A father, who has to remain anonymous, in a letter to the author.
9. *British Medical Journal*, 9 10 93, quoted in SANE's SANETALK, Winter 1993.
10. Dept of Health and Welsh Office, *CODE OF PRACTICE, Mental Health Act 1983, 1993.* See especially p.iii and p.6.

## Chapter 7

1. Falloon, I and Talbot, R, 'Achieving the goals of day treatment', *Journal of Nervous and Mental Diseases*, Vol 170, No 5 (1981) 279–85.
2. For overviews of research see (a) David, J M 'Overview: maintence therapy in psychiatry', *American Journal of Psychiatry*, 132 (1975), 237–245 and (b) Richard Wyatt, 'Neuroleptics and the Natural Course of Schizophrenia' *Schizophrenia Bulletin*, (1991)Vol 17, No 2.
3. See (2b) above, p.347.
4. Naomi Smith, *New Prospects for Schizophrenia* 1987; Kera Press, 27 Altenburg Avenue, London, W13 9RN.
5. See letter printed in the NSF Newsletter, May, 1987, quoted in Gwen Howe, *The Reality of Schizophrenia*, London: Faber & Faber 1991.
6. World Health Organization, 'Schizophrenia: An International Follow-up Study', Wiley, London, 1979, quoted by Max Birchwood *et al.* 'Predicting

relapse in schizophrenia; the development and implementation of an early signs monitoring system using patients and families as observers, a preliminary investigation, *Psychological Medicine*, 1989, 19, 649–656.

## Chapter 9

1. Ferris, J and Wilson, F, 'Schizophrenia: opening the door', *Social Work Today*, 27th October 1988, p. 27, quoted in Gwen Howe, *The Reality of Schizophrenia*, London: Faber & Faber 1991.

2. West Midlands RHA (1991) *Report of the Panel of Inquiry Appointed to Investigate the Case of Kim Kirkman.*

## Chapter 10

1. See Census 1991, OPCS, quoted in South Essex Health, *Shaping Mental Health Services*, January 1994.

## Chapter 11

1. Described in *Schizophrenia: A Fresh Approach*, David & Charles, 1986 & 1990, and *The Reality of Schizophrenia*, Faber & Faber, 1991.

2. Dohan, F 'Schizophrenia and neuroactive peptides from food', *The Lancet*, 1 (1979), 1031.

3. For example, see (a) Zioudrou, C, Streaty, R and Klee W, 'Opioid peptides derived from food proteins; the exorphins', *Journal of Biological Chemistry*, 254 (1979), 2446–9, and (b) Wood, N *et al.* 'Abnormal intestinal permeability – an aetiological factor in chronic psychiatric disorders?', *British Journal of Psychiatry*, 150 (1987), 853–6.

## Chapter 13

1. Rachel Perkins and Sarah Dilks, 'Worlds apart: Working with severely socially disabled people', *Journal of Mental Health* (1992) 1, 3–17.

2. F Jenner, A Monteiro, J Zegalo-Cardoso & J Cunha-Oliveira, *Schizophrenia*, Sheffield Academic Press, as quoted in review 'Double Take on Schizophrenia' by John McCrone, science writer, *New Scientist*, 12 1 94

3. Jo Smith and Max Birchwood, 'Relatives and Patients as Partners in the Management of Schizophrenia: The Development of a Service Model', *British Journal of Psychiatry* (1990), 156, 654–660.

4. Edwina Currie, when Junior Minister of Health with special responsibilities for the mentally ill, speaking at the 1988 MIND annual conference, reported in *Social Work Today*, 8th December 1988.

5. Mary Tyler, from an unpublished survey carried out amongst members of the National Schizophrenia Fellowship, 1986.

6. G Carstairs, D Early, H Rollin & J Wing, Medical Advisers to the National Schizophrenia Fellowship, *The Bulletin of the Royal College of Psychiatrists*, 9, 3, pp. 59–60 (March 1985) quoted in *Schizophrenia: A Fresh Approach*, David & Charles, 1986.

7. Sally Cooper and Gwen Howe, unpublished survey carried out with members of local NSF Group, Spring 1993.

8. Max Birchwood, Jo Smith *et al.* 'Predicting relapse in schizophrenia: the development and implementation of an early signs monitoring system using patients and families as observers, a preliminary investigation', *Psychological Medicine*, 1989, 19, 649–656.

9. See (3) above.

10. *Mental Health Act 1983*, HMSO publication, Part II.

11. See, for example, (a) Richard Wyatt, 'Neuroleptics and the Natural Course of Schizophrenia', *Schizophrenia Bulletin*, Volume 17, No 2, 1991, and (b) Crow T, *et al. The Northwick Park Study of First Episodes of Schizophrenia* Part II: 'A randomized controlled trial of prophylactic neuroleptic treatment', *British Journal of Psychiatry*, 148 (1986), 120–7.

12. Jones, Kathleen, *Experience in Mental Health* (London: Sage Publications, 1988) p.97.

13. World Schizophrenia Fellowship; *Manual on Schizophrenia: A Guide for Families*, 1991.

# Useful Addresses

**Concern for the Mentally Ill**
30 Arkwright Road
London NW3 6BH
Tel: 081 883 8533
A registered charity 'to promote and protect the welfare of the mentally disordered' and to provide a united voice for professionals involved in the care, treatment and rehabilitation of mentally vulnerable people.

**Disability Alliance**
25 Denmark Street
London WC2H 8NJ
Publishes a comprehensive handbook on benefits and allowances for the disabled, updated annually.

**Making Space**
46 Allen Street
Warrington
Cheshire WA2 7JB
Tel: 0925 571680
Concerned with assisting sufferers and families in the North of England and promoting community care facilities and education.

**National Schizophrenia Fellowship, (NSF)**
28 Castle Street
Kingston-upon-Thames
Surrey KT1 1SS
Tel: 081 547 3937
Concerned with helping those affected by serious mental illness, with improving services and promoting education and knowledge. Regular newsletters and conferences. Local self-help groups throughout the country. For information on these and other NSF services in any particular area, ring the above telephone number for details of Regional offices.

**SANE: Schizophrenia a National Emergency**
199–205, Old Marylebone Road
London NW1 5QP
Tel: 071 724 6520
Now concerned with all serious mental illness; provides telephone helpline
– 071–724–8000 – during afternoons, evenings and weekends. Raises funds
for research, campaigning and promoting knowledge. Newsletter.

**Schizophrenia Association of Great Britain (SAGB)**
International Schizophrenia Centre
Bryn Hyfryd
The Crescent
Bangor
Gwynedd LL57 2AG
Tel: 0248 354048
Concerned with helping those trying to cope with schizophrenia. Raises
funds for own ongoing biological research based at Bangor University.
Newsletter.

**The ZITO Trust**
P.O. Box 265
London WC2H 9JD
Tel: 071 240 2326
Concerned with advocating for the victims of the failure of Commnity Care
policy and campaigning for better services for the severely mentally ill whose
condition can pose a threat to themselves and to others. This new trust is
actively seeking financial support to achieve its aims and objectives.

# Further Reading

*A TRAGEDY OF SCHIZOPHRENIA: The Wife's Tale* by Fiona McDonald, ed.ited by Henry R. Rollin (National Schizophrenia Fellowship – see under Useful Addresses)

Published in the 1970s, this book continues to be frequently recommended by those who read it. It reveals how a second, untreated, episode of schizophrenia led to the break-up of a marriage and to the sick husband living an isolated life in a bedsitter because those who could help turned the other way. The book is made up of the wife's extended correspondence with all the various parties involved in her attempts to get help for her husband. Her experiences are summed up with the words 'there is no consideration for illness by my husband's solicitor – he once wrote it was irrelevant'.

*CODE OF PRACTICE:* Mental Health Act 1983 – Department of Health and Welsh Office (HMSO August 1993)

The most recent edition of the Code of Practice really should be mandatory reading for all professionals who work with the seriously mentally ill and it should be readily available, together with the Mental Health Act 1983, for all service providers working in this field. Also useful for families caught up in a crisis situation which may call for resort to the law.

*EXPERIENCE IN MENTAL HEALTH: Community Care and Social Policy* by Kathleen Jones (Sage 1988)

This book gives an illuminating overview of different models of community care in various parts of the world and highlights the problems of embarking on new policies without first carrying out appropriate research.

*HOMELESSNESS AND MENTAL ILLNESS: The Dark Side of Community Care* Edited by Martin Page and Robin Powell (Concern Publications, 52 Friern Barnet Road, London N11 3BP; 1991)

This small book includes contributions from some of those at the 'sharp end' of community care such as representatives of St Mungo association, the Salvation Army and The Simon Community. See 'Concern for the Mentally Ill' under useful addresses.

*LIVING WITH MENTAL ILLNESS* by Liz Kuipers and Paul Bebbington (Souvenir Press Ltd, Human Horizons Series, 1987)

This is a book for relatives of the mentally ill. Families trying to cope with a schizophrenic illness should find much of it informative and relevant to their own situation.

*NOWHERE TO GO* by E Fuller Torrey (Harper & Row 1988)

This is a searing indictment of the plight of the seriously mentally ill in the United States. This was the book which should have stemmed the enthusiasm in other countries to rush down the same road. It didn't!

*SCHIZOPHRENIA: A Fresh Approach* by Gwen Howe (David & Charles 2nd edition, 1990)

Useful general introduction by the present author, which includes chapters on mental health law, community resources and a detailed discussion on a dietary approach to schizophrenia. No longer in print, but available in public libraries (with around 35,000 borrowings since the first edition was published in 1986) and also from the NSF, SAGB and SAI – see under Useful Addresses.

*SCHIZOPHRENIA AT HOME* by Clare Greer and·John Wing (National Schizophrenia Fellowship; 2nd edition, 1988)

This second edition of a book first published in 1974 clearly demonstrates that little has changed since that time for families trying to cope with this illness. The first edition represented an innovative decision to reveal the experiences of relatives of sufferers and to present these in a 'plain and unvarnished way'. The book is still a valuable source of information twenty years on.

*SCHIZOPHRENIA: The Facts* by Ming T. Tsuang (Oxford University Press, 1992)

This is a refreshingly straightforward, brief, account of the basics of a schizophrenic illness, representing an ideal introduction to this complex subject.

*SCHIZOPHRENIA FROM WITHIN* Edited by John Wing (National Schizophrenia Fellowship; 1975)

This small book continues to represent a unique introduction to the strange experiences of a schizophrenic illness. Seven sufferers share their stories with us and their accounts are as compelling reading today as when I first discovered the book in the late 1970s.

*SCHIZOPHRENIA: Voices in the Dark* by Mary Moate and David Enoch (Kingsway Publications, c/o 1 St Anne's Road, Eastbourne, East Sussex; 1990)

A Christian sufferer has written 'much fear and guilt is evident and breakdown can be interpreted as failure to be a good Christian'. She feels this book has much to offer all those in the Church trying to grapple with this dilemma. It is a readable and compassionate contribution by a mother of a schizophrenic son and by a psychiatrist who has worked with this type of illness for over thirty-five years. It is also a useful introduction to this whole subject.

*STANLEY AND THE WOMEN* by Kingsley Amis (Penguin Books, 1989)

This gem of a book represents a welcome opportunity quite painlessly to gain an understanding of what can happen to families seeking help with this illness. Written with the author's customary brand of wit and cynicism, it nevertheless 'gets it right', with a subtle amusing approach quite absent in the television dramatization of the book.

*SURVIVING SCHIZOPHRENIA* by E. Fuller Torrey (Harper & Row, 3rd edition, 1988)

This must be the most comprehensive coverage of schizophrenia available today, although this does not include specific details of the working of the system in this country. Written by a leading psychiatrist in the United States whose sister is a sufferer, the author is a prolific and outspoken writer on this subject with a readable down-to-earth approach.

*THE REALITY OF SCHIZOPHRENIA* by Gwen Howe (Faber & Faber, 1991)

This book, by the present author, sets out to explain the historical perspective and content of the ongoing academic debate about schizophrenia and to demonstrate its irrelevance to the everyday problems of sufferers and carers. In doing this, it covers most of the important aspects of coping with this illness.

*WELCOME SILENCE* by Carol North, M.D. (Simon & Schuster, hb, 1987. Arrow Books, pb, )

This is a courageous and dramatic 'blow-by-blow' account of this woman's struggle with schizophrenia during her teens and the time she was studying to become a doctor. She is a practising psychiatrist in the United States and must be one of the very first sufferers in the public eye who has 'come out' and told her story for the benefit of other sufferers.

# Index